COMBUST MOON

PART III

Himanshu
Shangari

INDIA • SINGAPORE • MALAYSIA

ISBN 979-8-88815-648-3

Om Namah Shivaay

This book has become possible with the Grace of Lord Shiva, and each valuable word in it is due to his blessings.

Om Namah Shivaay

Contents

They Come First *vii*

Prelude *ix*

1. Combust Moon in Seventh House in Aries 1
2. Combust Moon in Seventh House in Taurus 6
3. Combust Moon in Seventh House in Gemini 11
4. Combust Moon in Seventh House in Cancer 16
5. Combust Moon in Seventh House in Leo 21
6. Combust Moon in Seventh House in Virgo 26
7. Combust Moon in Seventh House in Libra 31
8. Combust Moon in Seventh House in Scorpio 36
9. Combust Moon in Seventh House in Sagittarius 41
10. Combust Moon in Seventh House in Capricorn 46
11. Combust Moon in Seventh House in Aquarius 51
12. Combust Moon in Seventh House in Pisces 56
13. Combust Moon in Eighth House in Aries 61
14. Combust Moon in Eighth House in Taurus 66
15. Combust Moon in Eighth House in Gemini 71
16. Combust Moon in Eighth House in Cancer 76
17. Combust Moon in Eighth House in Leo 81
18. Combust Moon in Eighth House in Virgo 86

19. Combust Moon in Eighth House in Libra 91
20. Combust Moon in Eighth House in Scorpio 96
21. Combust Moon in Eighth House in Sagittarius 101
22. Combust Moon in Eighth House in Capricorn 106
23. Combust Moon in Eighth House in Aquarius 111
24. Combust Moon in Eighth House in Pisces 116
25. Combust Moon in Ninth House in Aries 121
26. Combust Moon in Ninth House in Taurus 126
27. Combust Moon in Ninth House in Gemini 131
28. Combust Moon in Ninth House in Cancer 136
29. Combust Moon in Ninth House in Leo 140
30. Combust Moon in Ninth House in Virgo 145
31. Combust Moon in Ninth House in Libra 150
32. Combust Moon in Ninth House in Scorpio 155
33. Combust Moon in Ninth House in Sagittarius 160
34. Combust Moon in Ninth House in Capricorn 165
35. Combust Moon in Ninth House in Aquarius 170
36. Combust Moon in Ninth House in Pisces 175
Contact Details *181*

They Come First

After bowing to Lord Shiva, let me take this moment to bow to the person who has been a strong and supportive influence in my life. She is my respected and adorable mother, **Smt. Jeewan Lata**. So much can be said about her contribution to my life, that a whole book can be written about it. However, I will simply say that even an ocean of words can't describe her true contribution to my life.

After that, I bow to my dear and respected father **Lt. Sh. Bodh Raj Shangari**. Though he left us when I was nine only, the mere fact that he along with my mother brought me to this world, makes me indebted to him for this life as well as for the lives to come. God bless your soul father, wherever you are. Though you are physically not with me, you are always there with me and in me, through all the sweet memories of my childhood, and you will always be.

Prelude

Vedic astrology is a very old and comprehensive faith of astrology. Though some other similar faiths are like streams or rivers, Vedic astrology is an ocean which can provide resources to many of these faiths. I have studied and researched many such faiths like Numerology and Vastu, but none of them holds its ground without the support of Vedic astrology. It is the faith which is the backbone of many such faiths.

The fact that Vedic astrology is among the oldest faiths of its kind, also makes it vulnerable to many types of corruptions and adulterations from time to time. Some of these adulterations may be the results of misinterpretations of various concepts of Vedic astrology from time to time. Some others may be there because some scholars may have twisted some definitions, for selfish motives. Due to such adulterations, corruptions and misinterpretations, Vedic astrology may not look as capable and accurate to some people, as it actually is.

With the grace of Lord Shiva, I have spent years in researching various concepts of Vedic astrology. It has been a constant effort to find out where and how much, such concepts may have been misinterpreted; and what could be the correct interpretations of these concepts. Though in their misinterpreted forms, most such concepts of Vedic astrology don't hold ground in real practice of astrology, almost all of them hold solid ground in their modified forms. This effort has taken many years of research, and analysis of thousands of horoscopes. The results, however, have been very rewarding.

This book is an effort to create awareness among the lovers of Vedic astrology that this faith is still as capable as it was when it was born. Various misinterpretations from time to time may have caused confusions related to several important concepts of this faith. Through this series of books, an attempt has been made to create awareness about the concept of Combust Moon.

When a planet comes closer to Sun, more than a safer distance to be maintained, such planet may become weaker as Sun may burn out some of its strength. Such planet that loses some of its strength by virtue of being too close to Sun is called a combust planet. It means when such planet happens to be Moon, it is called combust Moon.

Such combination of Sun and combust Moon can produce a wide variety of results in various houses of horoscope, depending on benefic/malefic nature of these two planets, their signs as well as nakshatras of placements, and on the overall theme of the horoscope under consideration.

This book deals with the placements of Combust Moon in the 7th, 8th and 9th houses of horoscope. Individual chapters have been assigned to Combust Moon in each one of these houses, in different signs. Benefic as well as malefic effects of Combust Moon have been discussed in each one of these houses in different signs, along with relevant examples from horoscopes.

Lord Shiva Bless You

– Himanshu Shangari

Combust Moon in Seventh House in Aries

When Sun and combust Moon are placed in the seventh house of a horoscope in Aries, Libra rises in the ascendant. Sun rules the eleventh house, and Moon rules the tenth house. In general, this combination is benefic here, in most cases. The concept of various planets exhibiting tendencies to be benefic or malefic on the basis of the houses they rule in a horoscope has been explained in the book 'Gemstones: Magic or Science?'.

Combination of Sun and combust Moon in the seventh house of horoscope in Aries is benefic in most cases, though it may turn malefic in some cases. It may happen when such combination is influenced by one or more malefic planets, and/or an overall malefic horoscope. The concept of a benefic planet turning malefic due to influences of malefic planets has been explained in the book 'Match Making and Manglik Dosh'.

When benefic in nature, combination of Sun and combust Moon in the seventh house of a horoscope in Aries can bless the native with good results related to father, mother, friends, marriage, husband, wife, profession, finances, reputation, authority, recognition, fame and several other good results, depending on his/her overall horoscope and running times.

Such combination of Sun and combust Moon can render various types of benefits to the native, related to or through his father, mother, marriage and/or friends. Considering parents, native's father/mother may be a rich man/woman, a celebrity, an officer in government or a powerful politician. The native may enjoy many benefits because of his father/mother's money, influence and/or status. He/she may give a big amount of money, and/or wealth to the native, while he/she's alive, and/or through his/her will. Considering marriage, the native may witness several benefits due to or through his wife and/or her family members. Considering friends, some of his friends may stand by the native and they may help him get out of his problems, many times in his life.

Looking at profession, such combust Moon can help the native achieve success as a fire fighter, fitness trainer, body builder, sportsman, athlete, physician, dietician, lawyer, astrologer, tantric, psychic, spiritual guru, healer, religious guru, teacher, preacher, consultant, actor, singer, musician, writer, dancer, sportsman, artist, architect, designer, developer, poet, chef, interior designer, host, researcher, analyst, professional dealing in education industry, coaching, food, health, pharma, medical, nursing, homecare, real estate, agriculture, hospitality, beauty, fashion, finance, television, music, sports, media, book, publishing, fitness, travel, hotel, airline, fishing, shipping, telecom, computer, software, IT, internet industry or some other type of professional, depending on his/her overall horoscope and running times.

Taking an example for a female native, suppose benefic combust Moon is placed in the seventh house of a horoscope in Aries with benefic exalted Sun. Retrograde Venus is placed in the sixth house in Pisces with debilitated Mercury; benefic Rahu is placed in the eleventh house in Leo, Ketu is placed in the fifth house in Aquarius, and benefic Saturn is placed in the fourth house in Capricorn with debilitated Jupiter. Saturn forms Shasha Yoga in the fourth house. In this case, the native may become a scientist, she may specialize in molecular biology, and she may witness good results.

If benefic Mars is placed in the ninth house in Gemini, the equation may become better. The native may possess remarkable knowledge of her field, and she may come across very good amount of success and recognition, along with good amount of money and fame. She may conduct research, and she may come across discoveries. If the finer factors and running times are supportive, she may become one of the most recognized scientists of her time. She may receive several awards, including a Nobel prize.

Such combust Moon can bless the native with authority in government as a police officer, army, air force, naval, revenue, administrative, foreign services officer, judge, doctor, scientist, engineer, politician or some other type of professional. Taking an example, suppose benefic combust Moon is placed in the seventh house of a horoscope in Aries with Venus, Mercury and benefic exalted Sun. Benefic retrograde Mars is placed in twelfth house in Virgo, benefic exalted Rahu is placed in the eighth house in Taurus, exalted Ketu is placed in the second house in Scorpio, and exalted Jupiter is placed in the tenth house in Cancer. In this case, the native may become an officer in administrative services, and he may enjoy a good career.

If benefic Saturn forms Shasha Yoga in the fourth house in Capricorn, the equation may become better. In this case, the native may achieve success in civil exams, and he may get selected for the highest possible direct rank in administrative services. He may serve at several important posts during his career, and he may come across very good amount of success, recognition and authority. If the finer factors and running times are supportive, he may serve as the head of an administrative department, before retirement.

On the other hand, when malefic in nature, combination of Sun and combust Moon in the seventh house of a horoscope in Aries can trouble the native with problems related to father, mother, friends, marriage, husband, wife, profession, finances, reputation, authority, recognition and several other problems, depending on his/her overall horoscope and running times.

Sun rules the eleventh house, Moon rules the tenth house, and they are placed in the seventh house. If such combination of Sun and combust Moon is influenced by malefic planets, and/or an overall malefic horoscope, the native may witness various types of problems related to or through his father, mother, marriage and/or friends. Considering parents, the native may not have a good equation with his father/mother, his parents may get divorced and he may live with his father/mother, his father/mother may suffer from a long-lasting illness, he/she may be an alcoholic and/or a drug addict, he/she may be a criminal, and/or he/she may die before native's age of 20, depending on native's overall horoscope and running times. Considering marriage, the native may witness delay/disturbances in marriage, and/or one or more failed marriages. He may have serious differences of opinion with his wife, she may suffer from a long-lasting illness, she may be an alcoholic and/or a drug addict, she may be a criminal, she may not be loyal to him, she may have extramarital affair/affairs, and/or she may die within 10 or 5 years of marriage. Considering friends, some of his friends may be selfish, opportunists, criminal-minded, criminals, drug addicts, traitors and/or they may have some other negative traits. The native may witness several problems because of such friends, many times in his life.

The native may witness delays, financial losses, setbacks, failures, job loss, bad reputation and several other problems related to or through his profession. Taking an example, suppose combust Moon is placed in the seventh house of a horoscope in Aries with exalted Sun, malefic retrograde Jupiter and malefic Ketu. Malefic Rahu is placed in the first house in Libra, exalted Venus is placed in the sixth house in Pisces with debilitated Mercury; Saturn is placed in the eighth house in Taurus, and Mars is placed in the twelfth house in Virgo. Grahan Yoga and Guru Chandal Yoga are formed in the seventh house.

In this case, native's father may die before native's age of 10/5, and his mother may die before his age of 20/15. He may not find a permanent profession till his age of 35/40, or throughout his life, though he may earn well at times. He may remain jobless for periods of more than 3 months, many times in his life. He may lose one or more good friends to death, before his age of 35/30. He may witness 1 or 2 failed marriages.

Combust Moon in Seventh House in Taurus

When Sun and combust Moon are placed in the seventh house of a horoscope in Taurus, Scorpio rises in the ascendant. Sun rules the tenth house, and Moon rules the ninth house. In general, this combination is benefic here, in most cases. The concept of various planets exhibiting tendencies to be benefic or malefic on the basis of the houses they rule in a horoscope has been explained in the book 'Gemstones: Magic or Science?'.

Combination of Sun and combust Moon in the seventh house of horoscope in Taurus is benefic in most cases, though it may turn malefic in some cases. It may happen when such combination is influenced by one or more malefic planets, and/or an overall malefic horoscope. The concept of a benefic planet turning malefic due to influences of malefic planets has been explained in the book 'Match Making and Manglik Dosh'.

When benefic in nature, combination of Sun and combust Moon in the seventh house of a horoscope in Taurus can bless the native with good results related to father, mother, creativity, marriage, husband, wife, profession, finances, reputation, authority, recognition, fame and several other good results, depending on his/her overall horoscope and running times.

Such combination of Sun and combust Moon can render various types of benefits to the native, related to or through his father, mother and/or marriage. Considering parents, native's

father/mother may be a rich man/woman, a celebrity, an officer in government or a powerful politician. The native may enjoy many benefits because of his father/mother's money, influence and/or status. He/she may give a big amount of money, and/or wealth to the native, while he/she's alive, and/or through his/her will. Considering marriage, the native may get married to a woman who may be beautiful, rich, a celebrity, an officer in government, a powerful politician, a successful businesswoman, and/or a citizen of a foreign country. The native may witness several benefits due to or through his wife and/or her family members.

Looking at profession, such combust Moon can help the native achieve success as a fire fighter, fitness trainer, body builder, sportsman, athlete, physician, dietician, lawyer, astrologer, tantric, psychic, spiritual guru, healer, religious guru, teacher, preacher, consultant, researcher, analyst, host, artist, poet, chef, interior designer, police officer, army, air force, naval, revenue, administrative, foreign services officer, judge, doctor, scientist, engineer, politician, professional dealing in education industry, coaching, food, health, pharma, medical, nursing, homecare, real estate, agriculture, hospitality, beauty, fashion, finance, television, music, sports, media, book, publishing, fitness, travel, hotel, airline, fishing, shipping, telecom, computer, software, IT, internet industry or some other type of professional, depending on his/her overall horoscope and running times.

Taking an example, suppose benefic combust Moon is placed in the seventh house of a horoscope in Taurus with Venus and benefic Sun. Benefic Mercury is placed in the sixth house in Aries with Jupiter; benefic Rahu is placed in the fourth house in Aquarius, Ketu is placed in the tenth house in Leo, and retrograde Mars is placed in the twelfth house in Libra. In this case, the native may start a retail supermarket, and he may witness good results.

If benefic retrograde Saturn is placed in the eleventh house in Virgo, the equation may become better. In this case, the native may come across very good amount of success, money and recognition through retail industry. His business may expand after his age of 35/40, and it may keep growing. If the finer factors and running times are supportive, he may own a chain of retail supermarkets worth in billions, by his age of 55/60.

Such combust Moon can help the native achieve success through a creative field as an actor, singer, musician, writer, dancer, sportsman, artist, architect, designer, developer or some other likewise professional. Taking an example for female native, suppose benefic combust Moon is placed in the seventh house of a horoscope in Taurus with Mercury and benefic Sun. Benefic Rahu is placed in the second house in Sagittarius with Mars; Ketu is placed in the eighth house in Gemini, exalted Venus is placed in the fifth house in Pisces, and benefic retrograde Saturn is placed in the ninth house in Cancer. In this case, the native may become a singer, and she may witness good results.

If benefic retrograde Jupiter is placed in the eleventh house in Virgo, the equation may become better. The native may possess remarkable singing talent, and she may come across very good amount of success, money, recognition and fame. She may deliver several hit songs, and she may receive many awards. If the finer factors and running times are supportive, she may become one of the most successful singers of her time, and her net worth may be in multimillions.

On the other hand, when malefic in nature, combination of Sun and combust Moon in the seventh house of a horoscope in Taurus can trouble the native with problems related to father, mother, marriage, husband, wife, profession, finances, reputation, authority, recognition and several other problems, depending on his/her overall horoscope and running times.

Sun rules the tenth house, Moon rules the ninth house, and they are placed in the seventh house. If such combination of Sun and combust Moon is influenced by malefic planets, and/or an overall malefic horoscope, the native may witness various types of problems related to or through his father, mother and/or marriage. Considering parents, the native may not have a good equation with his father/mother, his parents may get divorced and he may live with his father/mother, his father/mother may suffer from a long-lasting illness, he/she may be an alcoholic and/or a drug addict, he/she may be a criminal, and/or he/she may die before native's age of 20, depending on native's overall horoscope and running times. Considering marriage, the native may witness delay/disturbances in marriage, and/or one or more failed marriages. He may have serious differences of opinion with his wife, she may suffer from a long-lasting illness, she may be an alcoholic and/or a drug addict, she may be a criminal, she may not be loyal to him, she may have extramarital affair/affairs, and/or she may die within 10 or 5 years of marriage.

The native may witness delays, financial losses, setbacks, failures, job loss, bad reputation and several other problems related to or through his profession. Taking an example, suppose combust Moon is placed in the seventh house of a horoscope in Taurus with Sun, malefic retrograde Mercury and malefic Venus. Malefic Rahu and Jupiter form Guru Chandal Yoga in the sixth house in Aries, malefic Ketu is placed in the twelfth house in Libra with Saturn; and Mars is placed in the fourth house in Aquarius.

In this case, native's father as well as mother may die before his age of 15/10. He may not find a permanent profession throughout his life, and he may only find temporary jobs. He may witness financial tightness and debts, many times in his life. He may remain jobless for periods of more than 3 months, many times in his life. He may lose one or more good friends to death, before his age of 35/30. He may witness 1 or 2 failed marriages.

Combust Moon in Seventh House in Gemini

When Sun and combust Moon are placed in the seventh house of a horoscope in Gemini, Sagittarius rises in the ascendant. Sun rules the ninth house, and Moon rules the eighth house. In general, this combination is partly benefic and partly malefic here, though the malefic part is higher, in most cases. The concept of various planets exhibiting tendencies to be benefic or malefic on the basis of the houses they rule in a horoscope has been explained in the book 'Gemstones: Magic or Science?'.

Combination of Sun and combust Moon in the seventh house of horoscope in Gemini is malefic in many cases, though it may turn benefic in some cases. It may happen when such combination is influenced by one or more benefic planets, and/or an overall benefic horoscope. The concept of a malefic planet turning benefic due to influences of benefic planets has been explained in the book 'Match Making and Manglik Dosh'.

When benefic in nature, combination of Sun and combust Moon in the seventh house of a horoscope in Gemini can bless the native with good results related to father, mother, creativity, marriage, husband, wife, profession, finances, reputation, authority, recognition, fame and several other good results, depending on his/her overall horoscope and running times.

Such combination of Sun and combust Moon can render various types of benefits to the native, related to or through his

father, mother and/or marriage. Considering parents, native's father/mother may be a rich man/woman, a celebrity, an officer in government or a powerful politician. The native may enjoy many benefits because of his father/mother's money, influence and/or status. He/she may give a big amount of money, and/or wealth to the native, while he/she's alive, and/ or through his/her will. Considering marriage, the native may get married to a woman who may be beautiful, rich, a celebrity, an officer in government, a powerful politician, a successful businesswoman, and/or a citizen of a foreign country. The native may witness several benefits due to or through his wife and/or her family members.

Looking at profession, such combust Moon can help the native achieve success as a fire fighter, fitness trainer, body builder, sportsman, athlete, physician, dietician, lawyer, astrologer, tantric, psychic, spiritual guru, healer, religious guru, teacher, preacher, consultant, researcher, analyst, host, artist, poet, chef, interior designer, professional dealing in education industry, coaching, food, health, pharma, medical, nursing, homecare, real estate, agriculture, hospitality, beauty, fashion, finance, television, music, sports, media, book, publishing, fitness, travel, hotel, airline, fishing, shipping, telecom, computer, software, IT, internet industry or some other type of professional, depending on his/her overall horoscope and running times.

Such combust Moon can help the native achieve success through a creative field as an actor, singer, musician, writer, dancer, sportsman, artist, architect, designer, developer or some other likewise professional. Taking an example, suppose combust Moon is placed in the seventh house of a horoscope in Gemini with Mars, Venus, benefic Sun and benefic retrograde Mercury. Benefic debilitated Rahu is placed in the fourth house in Pisces, debilitated Ketu is placed in the tenth house in Virgo, and benefic debilitated Saturn is placed in the fifth house in Aries. Mercury forms Bhadra Yoga in the seventh house whereas Sun and Mercury form Budhaditya Yoga in the same house. In this case, the native may become a footballer, and he may witness good results.

If benefic Jupiter is placed in the ninth house in Leo, the equation may become better. The native may possess remarkable talent related to the sport, and he may come across very good amount of success, money, recognition and fame. He may deliver several match winning performances, and he may receive many awards/medals. If the finer factors and running times are supportive, he may become one of the greatest footballers of all time, and his net worth may be in multimillions.

Such combust Moon can bless the native with authority in government as a police officer, army, air force, naval, revenue, administrative, foreign services officer, judge, doctor, scientist, engineer, politician or some other type of professional. Taking an example, suppose combust Moon is placed in the seventh house of a horoscope in Gemini with retrograde Venus, benefic retrograde Mercury and benefic Sun. Benefic exalted Rahu is placed in the sixth house in Taurus with Mars; and benefic retrograde Saturn is placed in the twelfth house in Scorpio with exalted Ketu. Budhaditya Yoga and Bhadra Yoga are formed in the seventh house. In this case, the native may become an officer in army, and he may enjoy a good career.

If benefic Jupiter is placed in the tenth house in Virgo, the equation may become better. In this case, the native may achieve success in competitive exams, and he may get selected for the highest possible direct rank in army. He may serve at several important posts during his career, and he may come across very good amount of success, recognition and authority. If the finer factors and running times are supportive, he may serve as the chief of army of his country, before retirement.

On the other hand, when malefic in nature, combination of Sun and combust Moon in the seventh house of a horoscope in Gemini can trouble the native with problems related to father, mother, lifespan, marriage, husband, wife, profession, finances, reputation, authority, recognition and several other problems, depending on his/her overall horoscope and running times.

Sun rules the ninth house, Moon rules the eighth house, and they are placed in the seventh house. If such combination of Sun and combust Moon is influenced by malefic planets, and/or an overall malefic horoscope, the native may witness various types of problems related to or through his father, mother, marriage and/or lifespan. Considering parents, the native may not have a good equation with his father/mother, his parents may get divorced and he may live with his father/mother, his father/mother may suffer from a long-lasting illness, he/she may be an alcoholic and/or a drug addict, he/she may be a criminal, and/or he/she may die before native's age of 20, depending on native's overall horoscope and running times. Considering marriage, the native may witness delay/disturbances in marriage, and/or one or more failed marriages. He may have serious differences of opinion with his wife, she may suffer from a long-lasting illness, she may be an alcoholic and/or a drug addict, she may be a criminal, she may not be loyal to him, she may have extramarital affair/

affairs, and/or she may die within 10 or 5 years of marriage. Considering lifespan, the native may witness reduction in lifespan due to several reasons. For example, the native may die in an accident, through a natural disaster, due to a fatal disease, due to a fatal viral infection like COVID, due to drug addiction, he may commit suicide, or someone may kill him intentionally or unintentionally.

The native may witness delays, financial losses, setbacks, failures, job loss, bad reputation and several other problems related to or through his profession. Taking an example, suppose malefic combust Moon is placed in the seventh house of a horoscope in Gemini with Sun and malefic Mars. Malefic Venus is placed in the sixth house in Taurus with Mercury; malefic Rahu is placed in the ninth house in Leo, malefic Ketu is placed in the third house in Aquarius, benefic Saturn is placed in the fourth house in Pisces, and Jupiter is placed in the twelfth house in Scorpio.

In this case, native's father may die before native's age of 10 or 5. His mother may get married again, but the native may not have a good equation with his stepfather. He may not achieve much professional success till his age of 35/40, or throughout his life, though he may earn well at times. He may remain jobless for periods of more than 3 months, many times in his life. He may witness 1 or 2 failed marriages, and he may not get married after that. He may die before his age of 55/50, due to a heart attack, in an accident, or because of a fatal viral infection like COVID.

Combust Moon in Seventh House in Cancer

When Sun and combust Moon are placed in the seventh house of a horoscope in Cancer, Capricorn rises in the ascendant. Sun rules the eighth house, and Moon rules the seventh house. In general, this combination is partly benefic and partly malefic here, though the benefic part is higher, in most cases. The concept of various planets exhibiting tendencies to be benefic or malefic on the basis of the houses they rule in a horoscope has been explained in the book 'Gemstones: Magic or Science?'.

Combination of Sun and combust Moon in the seventh house of horoscope in Cancer is benefic in many cases, though it may turn malefic in some cases. It may happen when such combination is influenced by one or more malefic planets, and/or an overall malefic horoscope. The concept of a benefic planet turning malefic due to influences of malefic planets has been explained in the book 'Match Making and Manglik Dosh'.

When benefic in nature, combination of Sun and combust Moon in the seventh house of a horoscope in Cancer can bless the native with good results related to father, mother, marriage, husband, wife, profession, finances, reputation, authority, recognition, fame and several other good results, depending on his/her overall horoscope and running times.

Such combination of Sun and combust Moon can render various types of benefits to the native, related to or through his father, mother and/or marriage. Considering parents, native's father/mother may be a rich man/woman, a celebrity, an officer in government or a powerful politician. The native may enjoy many benefits because of his father/mother's money, influence and/or status. He/she may give a big amount of money, and/or wealth to the native, while he/she's alive, and/or through his/her will. Considering marriage, the native may get married to a woman who may be beautiful, rich, a celebrity, an officer in government, a powerful politician, a successful businesswoman, and/or a citizen of a foreign country. The native may witness several benefits due to or through his wife and/or her family members.

Looking at profession, such combust Moon can help the native achieve success as a fire fighter, fitness trainer, body builder, sportsman, athlete, physician, dietician, lawyer, astrologer, tantric, psychic, spiritual guru, healer, religious guru, teacher, preacher, consultant, researcher, analyst, host, artist, poet, chef, interior designer, professional dealing in education industry, coaching, food, health, pharma, medical, nursing, homecare, real estate, agriculture, hospitality, beauty, fashion, finance, television, music, sports, media, book, publishing, fitness, travel, hotel, airline, fishing, shipping, telecom, computer, software, IT, internet industry or some other type of professional, depending on his/her overall horoscope and running times.

Such combust Moon can help the native achieve success through a creative field as an actor, singer, musician, writer, dancer, sportsman, artist, architect, designer, developer or some other likewise professional. Taking an example, suppose benefic combust Moon is placed in the seventh house of a horoscope in Cancer with Mercury, Sun and benefic debilitated Mars. Benefic exalted Rahu is placed in the ninth house in Virgo, exalted Ketu is placed in the third house in Pisces, and benefic debilitated Saturn is placed in the fourth house in Aries with Jupiter. Moon and Mars form Neechbhang Rajyoga and Chandra Mangal Yoga in the seventh house. In this case, the native may become an actor, and he may witness good results.

If benefic Venus is placed in the fifth house in Taurus, the equation may become better. The native may possess remarkable acting talent, and he may come across very good amount of success, money, recognition and fame. He may act very well in the genres of drama, romance and action. He may deliver several hit movies, and he may receive many awards. If the finer factors and running times are supportive, he may become one of the most successful actors of his time, and his net worth may be in multimillions.

Such combust Moon can bless the native with authority in government as a police officer, army, air force, naval, revenue, administrative, foreign services officer, judge, doctor, scientist, engineer, politician or some other type of professional. Taking an example, suppose benefic combust Moon is placed in the seventh house of a horoscope in Cancer with Sun, Mercury and benefic Saturn. Benefic debilitated Venus is placed in the ninth house in Virgo with benefic exalted Rahu; exalted Ketu is placed in the third house in Pisces, and Jupiter is placed in the eighth house in Leo. Venus and Rahu form Neechbhang Rajyoga in the ninth house. In this case, the native may engage in politics, and he may become a member of parliament of his country.

If benefic Mars is placed in the tenth house in Libra, the equation may become better. In this case, the native may come across very good amount of success, recognition, authority and fame through politics. He may win several elections, and he may become a minister in national government. If the finer factors and running times are supportive, he may become minister, more than once.

On the other hand, when malefic in nature, combination of Sun and combust Moon in the seventh house of a horoscope in Cancer can trouble the native with problems related to father, mother, lifespan, marriage, husband, wife, profession, finances, reputation, authority, recognition and several other problems, depending on his/her overall horoscope and running times.

Sun rules the eighth house, Moon rules the seventh house, and they are placed in the seventh house. If such combination of Sun and combust Moon is influenced by malefic planets, and/or an overall malefic horoscope, the native may witness various types of problems related to or through his father, mother, marriage and/or lifespan. Considering parents, the native may not have a good equation with his father/mother, his parents may get divorced and he may live with his father/mother, his father/mother may suffer from a long-lasting illness, he/she may be an alcoholic and/or a drug addict, he/she may be a criminal, and/or he/she may die before native's age of 20, depending on native's overall horoscope and running times. Considering marriage, the native may witness delay/disturbances in marriage, and/or one or more failed marriages. He may have serious differences of opinion with his wife, she may suffer from a long-lasting illness, she may be an alcoholic and/or a drug addict, she may be a criminal, she may not be loyal to him, she may have extramarital affair/affairs, and/or she may die within 10 or 5 years of marriage. Considering lifespan, the native may witness reduction in lifespan due to several reasons. For example, the native may die in an accident, through a natural disaster, due to a fatal disease, due to a fatal viral infection like COVID, due to drug addiction, he may commit suicide, or someone may kill him intentionally or unintentionally.

The native may witness delays, financial losses, setbacks, failures, job loss, bad reputation and several other problems related to or through his profession. Taking an example, suppose combust Moon is placed in the seventh house of a horoscope in Cancer with malefic Sun and malefic Rahu. Malefic Ketu is placed in the first house in Capricorn with exalted Mars and malefic debilitated Jupiter; Venus is placed in the eighth house in Leo with retrograde Mercury; and Saturn is placed in the twelfth house in Sagittarius. Grahan Yoga is formed in the seventh house, and Guru Chandal Yoga is formed in the first house.

In this case, native's mother may die before his age of 10 or 5. His father may get married again, but the native may not have a good equation with his stepmother. He may not find a permanent profession throughout his life, and he may keep losing jobs, though he may earn well at times. He may remain jobless for periods of more than 6 months, many times in his life. He may witness 1 or 2 failed marriages.

Combust Moon in Seventh House in Leo

When Sun and combust Moon are placed in the seventh house of a horoscope in Leo, Aquarius rises in the ascendant. Sun rules the seventh house, and Moon rules the sixth house. In general, this combination is partly benefic and partly malefic here, though the benefic part is higher, in most cases. The concept of various planets exhibiting tendencies to be benefic or malefic on the basis of the houses they rule in a horoscope has been explained in the book 'Gemstones: Magic or Science?'.

Combination of Sun and combust Moon in the seventh house of horoscope in Leo is benefic in many cases, though it may turn malefic in some cases. It may happen when such combination is influenced by one or more malefic planets, and/or an overall malefic horoscope. The concept of a benefic planet turning malefic due to influences of malefic planets has been explained in the book 'Match Making and Manglik Dosh'.

When benefic in nature, combination of Sun and combust Moon in the seventh house of a horoscope in Leo can bless the native with good results related to father, mother, marriage, husband, wife, profession, finances, reputation, authority, recognition, fame and several other good results, depending on his/her overall horoscope and running times.

Such combination of Sun and combust Moon can render various types of benefits to the native, related to or through his

father, mother and/or marriage. Considering parents, native's father/mother may be a rich man/woman, a celebrity, an officer in government or a powerful politician. The native may enjoy many benefits because of his father/mother's money, influence and/or status. He/she may give a big amount of money, and/or wealth to the native, while he/she's alive, and/ or through his/her will. Considering marriage, the native may get married to a woman who may be beautiful, rich, a celebrity, an officer in government, a powerful politician, a successful businesswoman, and/or a citizen of a foreign country. The native may witness several benefits due to or through his wife and/or her family members.

Looking at profession, such combust Moon can help the native achieve success as a fire fighter, fitness trainer, body builder, sportsman, athlete, physician, dietician, lawyer, astrologer, tantric, psychic, spiritual guru, healer, religious guru, teacher, preacher, consultant, researcher, analyst, host, artist, poet, chef, interior designer, professional dealing in education industry, coaching, food, health, pharma, medical, nursing, homecare, real estate, agriculture, hospitality, beauty, fashion, finance, television, music, sports, media, book, publishing, fitness, travel, hotel, airline, fishing, shipping, telecom, computer, software, IT, internet industry or some other type of professional, depending on his/her overall horoscope and running times.

Such combust Moon can help the native achieve success through a creative field as an actor, singer, musician, writer, dancer, sportsman, artist, architect, designer, developer or some other likewise professional. Taking an example, suppose combust Moon is placed in the seventh house of a horoscope in Leo with Mercury and benefic Sun. Benefic Venus is placed in the fifth house in Gemini, benefic Mars is placed in the ninth house in Libra, benefic Rahu is placed in the sixth house in Cancer, Ketu is placed in the twelfth house in Capricorn, and Saturn is placed in the fourth house in Taurus. In this case, the native may write fictional books, and he may witness good results.

If benefic Jupiter is placed in the fifth house in Gemini with Venus, the equation may become better. The native may possess remarkable writing talent, and he may come across very good amount of success, money, recognition and fame. He may write in several genres, including drama and romance. He may deliver several bestsellers, and he may receive many awards. If the finer factors and running times are supportive, he may become one of the most successful writers of his time, and his net worth may be in multimillions.

Such combust Moon can bless the native with authority in government as a police officer, army, air force, naval, revenue, administrative, foreign services officer, judge, doctor, scientist, engineer, politician or some other type of professional. Taking an example, suppose combust Moon is placed in the seventh house of a horoscope in Leo with retrograde Mercury, benefic Sun and benefic Venus. Benefic Mars is placed in the third house in Aries with benefic Rahu; and Ketu is placed in the ninth house in Libra with Jupiter. In this case, the native may become an officer in air force, and he may enjoy a good career.

If retrograde Saturn is placed in the tenth house in Scorpio, the equation may become better. In this case, the native may achieve success in competitive exams, and he may get selected for the highest possible direct rank in air force. He may be a skilled fighter pilot, and he may succeed in several missions. He may serve at several important posts during his career, and he may come across very good amount of success, recognition and authority. If the finer factors and running times are supportive, he may serve at one of the top 2 ranks in air force, before retirement.

On the other hand, when malefic in nature, combination of Sun and combust Moon in the seventh house of a horoscope in Leo can trouble the native with problems related to father, mother, marriage, husband, wife, profession, finances, reputation, authority, recognition and several other problems, depending on his/her overall horoscope and running times.

Sun rules the seventh house, Moon rules the sixth house, and they are placed in the seventh house. If such combination of Sun and combust Moon is influenced by malefic planets, and/or an overall malefic horoscope, the native may witness various types of problems related to or through his father, mother and/or marriage. Considering parents, the native may not have a good equation with his father/mother, his parents may get divorced and he may live with his father/mother, his father/mother may suffer from a long-lasting illness, he/she may be an alcoholic and/or a drug addict, he/she may be a criminal, and/or he/she may die before native's age of 20, depending on native's overall horoscope and running times. Considering marriage, the native may witness delay/disturbances in marriage, and/or one or more failed marriages. He may have serious differences of opinion with his wife, she may suffer from a long-lasting illness, she may be an alcoholic and/or a drug addict, she may be a criminal, she may not be loyal to him, she may have extramarital affair/affairs, and/or she may die within 10 or 5 years of marriage.

The native may witness delays, financial losses, setbacks, failures, job loss, bad reputation and several other problems related to or through his profession. Taking an example, suppose malefic combust Moon is placed in the seventh house of a horoscope in Leo with Sun, retrograde Mercury and malefic Rahu. Malefic Ketu is placed in the first house in Aquarius with retrograde Jupiter; Venus is placed in the sixth house in Cancer with debilitated Mars; and Saturn is placed in the eighth house in Virgo. Grahan Yoga is formed in the seventh house whereas Guru Chandal Yoga is formed in the first house.

In this case, native's father may die before native's age of 15 or 10, and his mother may die before his age of 25 or 20. The native may not achieve much professional success till his age of 35/40, or throughout his life, though he may earn well at times. He may witness bad reputation and financial losses through profession. He may witness 2 or 3 failed marriages.

Combust Moon in Seventh House in Virgo

When Sun and combust Moon are placed in the seventh house of a horoscope in Virgo, Pisces rises in the ascendant. Sun rules the sixth house, and Moon rules the fifth house. In general, this combination is partly benefic and partly malefic here, though the benefic part is higher, in most cases. The concept of various planets exhibiting tendencies to be benefic or malefic on the basis of the houses they rule in a horoscope has been explained in the book 'Gemstones: Magic or Science?'.

Combination of Sun and combust Moon in the seventh house of horoscope in Virgo is benefic in many cases, though it may turn malefic in some cases. It may happen when such combination is influenced by one or more malefic planets, and/or an overall malefic horoscope. The concept of a benefic planet turning malefic due to influences of malefic planets has been explained in the book 'Match Making and Manglik Dosh'.

When benefic in nature, combination of Sun and combust Moon in the seventh house of a horoscope in Virgo can bless the native with good results related to father, mother, love life, children, creativity, marriage, husband, wife, profession, finances, reputation, authority, recognition, fame and several other good results, depending on his/her overall horoscope and running times.

Such combination of Sun and combust Moon can render various types of benefits to the native, related to or through his father, mother, marriage and/or children. Considering parents, native's father/mother may be a rich man/woman, a celebrity, an officer in government or a powerful politician. The native may enjoy many benefits because of his father/ mother's money, influence and/or status. He/she may give a big amount of money, and/or wealth to the native, while he/ she's alive, and/or through his/her will. Considering marriage, the native may get married to a woman who may be beautiful, rich, a celebrity, an officer in government, a powerful politician, a successful businesswoman, and/or a citizen of a foreign country. The native may witness several benefits due to or through his wife and/or her family members. Considering children, the native may have children who may be physically, intellectually, emotionally, creatively and/or spiritually better or much better than average. Such children may achieve a lot in many spheres of their lives, and they may bring good name and many other good results to the native.

Looking at profession, such combust Moon can help the native achieve success as a fire fighter, fitness trainer, body builder, sportsman, athlete, physician, dietician, lawyer, astrologer, tantric, psychic, spiritual guru, healer, religious guru, teacher, preacher, consultant, researcher, analyst, host, artist, poet, chef, interior designer, professional dealing in education industry, coaching, food, health, pharma, medical, nursing, homecare, real estate, agriculture, hospitality, beauty, fashion, finance, television, music, sports, media, book, publishing, fitness, travel, hotel, airline, fishing, shipping, telecom, computer, software, IT, internet industry or some other type of professional, depending on his/her overall horoscope and running times.

Such combust Moon can help the native achieve success through a creative field as an actor, singer, musician, writer, dancer, sportsman, artist, architect, designer, developer or some other likewise professional. Taking an example, suppose benefic combust Moon is placed in the seventh house of a horoscope in Virgo with Sun and benefic exalted Mercury. Venus is placed in the eighth house in Libra with exalted Saturn; benefic Jupiter is placed in the third house in Taurus with benefic Mars; benefic Rahu is placed in the fifth house in Cancer, and Ketu is placed in the eleventh house in Capricorn. Mercury forms Bhadra Yoga in the seventh house.

In this case, the native may become a music composer. He may possess remarkable talent, and he may come across very good amount of success, money, recognition and fame. He may compose music for several hit songs, and he may receive many awards. If the finer factors and running times are supportive, he may become one of the most successful music composers of his time, and his net worth may be in multimillions.

Such combust Moon can bless the native with authority in government as a police officer, army, air force, naval, revenue, administrative, foreign services officer, judge, doctor, scientist, engineer, politician or some other type of professional. Taking an example, suppose benefic combust Moon is placed in the seventh house of a horoscope in Virgo with Sun and benefic exalted Mercury. Venus is placed in the sixth house in Leo, benefic Rahu is placed in the eighth house in Libra, Ketu is placed in the second house in Aries, benefic Jupiter is placed in the ninth house in Scorpio, and benefic Mars is placed in the tenth house in Sagittarius with Saturn. Mercury forms Bhadra Yoga in the seventh house.

In this case, the native may achieve success in civil exams, and he may get selected for the highest possible direct rank in revenue services. He may serve at several important posts during his career, and he may come across very good amount of success, recognition and authority. If the finer factors and running times are supportive, he may serve as the head of a revenue department, before retirement.

On the other hand, when malefic in nature, combination of Sun and combust Moon in the seventh house of a horoscope in Virgo can trouble the native with problems related to father, mother, love life, children, marriage, husband, wife, profession, finances, reputation, authority, recognition and several other problems, depending on his/her overall horoscope and running times.

Sun rules the sixth house, Moon rules the fifth house, and they are placed in the seventh house. If such combination of Sun and combust Moon is influenced by malefic planets, and/or an overall malefic horoscope, the native may witness various types of problems related to or through his father, mother, marriage and/or children. Considering parents, the native may not have a good equation with his father/mother, his parents may get divorced and he may live with his father/ mother, his father/mother may suffer from a long-lasting illness, he/she may be an alcoholic and/or a drug addict, he/ she may be a criminal, and/or he/she may die before native's age of 20, depending on native's overall horoscope and running times. Considering marriage, the native may witness delay/disturbances in marriage, and/or one or more failed marriages. He may have serious differences of opinion with his wife, she may suffer from a long-lasting illness, she may be an alcoholic and/or a drug addict, she may be a criminal, she may not be loyal to him, she may have extramarital affair/

affairs, and/or she may die within 10 or 5 years of marriage. Considering children, the native may lose one or more children through miscarriages that his wife may witness. He may witness delay in childbirth, and/or he may have children who may be physically and/or mentally troubled in some way. He may lose his children through divorce, or his children may engage in immoral/illegal activities, and he may witness bad reputation and many other problems because of them. In an extreme case, the native may witness death of one or more children during their young ages.

The native may witness delays, financial losses, setbacks, failures, job loss, bad reputation and several other problems related to or through his profession. Taking an example, suppose combust Moon is placed in the seventh house of a horoscope in Virgo with malefic Sun, malefic debilitated Venus and malefic debilitated Ketu. Malefic debilitated Rahu is placed in the first house in Pisces, Mercury is placed in the sixth house in Leo with malefic retrograde Saturn; Jupiter is placed in the twelfth house in Aquarius, and Mars is placed in the eighth house in Libra. Grahan Yoga is formed in the seventh house.

In this case, native's mother may die before his age of 10 or 5, and his father may die before native's age of 20 or 15. The native may not find a permanent profession throughout his life, and he may keep losing jobs. He may remain jobless for periods of more than 3 months, many times in his life. He may not get married till his age of 35/40, or throughout his life. He may not have a child, till his age of 40/45, or throughout his life.

Combust Moon in Seventh House in Libra

When Sun and combust Moon are placed in the seventh house of a horoscope in Libra, Aries rises in the ascendant. Sun rules the fifth house, and Moon rules the fourth house. In general, this combination is benefic here, in most cases. The concept of various planets exhibiting tendencies to be benefic or malefic on the basis of the houses they rule in a horoscope has been explained in the book 'Gemstones: Magic or Science?'.

Combination of Sun and combust Moon in the seventh house of horoscope in Libra is benefic in most cases, though it may turn malefic in some cases. It may happen when such combination is influenced by one or more malefic planets, and/or an overall malefic horoscope. The concept of a benefic planet turning malefic due to influences of malefic planets has been explained in the book 'Match Making and Manglik Dosh'.

When benefic in nature, combination of Sun and combust Moon in the seventh house of a horoscope in Libra can bless the native with good results related to father, mother, education, wealth, properties, vehicles, love life, children, creativity, marriage, husband, wife, profession, finances, reputation, authority, recognition, fame and several other good results, depending on his/her overall horoscope and running times.

Such combination of Sun and combust Moon can render various types of benefits to the native, related to or through

his father, mother, marriage and/or children. Considering parents, native's father/mother may be a rich man/woman, a celebrity, an officer in government or a powerful politician. The native may enjoy many benefits because of his father/mother's money, influence and/or status. He/she may give a big amount of money, and/or wealth to the native, while he/she's alive, and/or through his/her will. This combination can bless the native with good education, vehicles, residential house/houses and/or several other good results. Considering marriage, the native may witness several benefits due to or through his wife and/or her family members. Considering children, the native may have children who may be physically, intellectually, emotionally, creatively and/or spiritually better or much better than average. Such children may achieve a lot in many spheres of their lives, and they may bring good name and many other good results to the native.

Looking at profession, such combust Moon can help the native achieve success as a fire fighter, fitness trainer, body builder, sportsman, athlete, physician, dietician, lawyer, astrologer, tantric, psychic, spiritual guru, healer, religious guru, teacher, preacher, consultant, researcher, analyst, host, artist, poet, chef, interior designer, professional dealing in education industry, coaching, food, health, pharma, medical, nursing, homecare, real estate, agriculture, hospitality, beauty, fashion, finance, television, music, sports, media, book, publishing, fitness, travel, hotel, airline, fishing, shipping, telecom, computer, software, IT, internet industry or some other type of professional, depending on his/her overall horoscope and running times.

Such combust Moon can help the native achieve success through a creative field as an actor, singer, musician, writer,

dancer, sportsman, artist, architect, designer, developer or some other likewise professional. Taking an example, suppose benefic combust Moon is placed in the seventh house of a horoscope in Libra with Mercury, benefic Venus and benefic debilitated Sun. Benefic exalted Rahu is placed in the second house in Taurus with retrograde Jupiter; exalted Ketu is placed in the eighth house in Scorpio, benefic retrograde Saturn is placed in the third house in Gemini, and Mars is placed in the fifth house in Leo. Sun and Venus form Neechbhang Rajyoga in the seventh house.

In this case, the native may become an actor. He may possess remarkable talent, and he may come across very good amount of success, money, recognition and fame. He may act very well in the genres of romance, drama, action and comedy. He may deliver several hit movies, and he may receive many awards. If the finer factors and running times are supportive, he may become one of the most successful actors of his time, and his net worth may be in multimillions.

Such combust Moon can bless the native with authority in government as a police officer, army, air force, naval, revenue, administrative, foreign services officer, judge, doctor, scientist, engineer, politician or some other type of professional. Taking another example, suppose benefic combust Moon is placed in the seventh house of a horoscope in Libra with Mercury and benefic debilitated Sun. Mars is placed in the fifth house in Leo with retrograde Jupiter; benefic Saturn is placed in the eleventh house in Aquarius, debilitated Venus is placed in the sixth house in Virgo, benefic Rahu is placed in the third house in Gemini, and Ketu is placed in the ninth house in Sagittarius.

In this case, the native may achieve success in civil exams, and he may get selected for the highest possible direct rank in foreign services. He may serve at several important posts during his career, and he may come across very good amount of success, recognition and authority. He may represent his country in several countries of the world. If the finer factors and running times are supportive, he may serve at one of the top 2 ranks in foreign services, before retirement.

On the other hand, when malefic in nature, combination of Sun and combust Moon in the seventh house of a horoscope in Libra can trouble the native with problems related to father, mother, education, wealth, properties, vehicles, love life, children, marriage, husband, wife, profession, finances, reputation, authority, recognition and several other problems, depending on his/her overall horoscope and running times.

Sun rules the fifth house, Moon rules the fourth house, and they are placed in the seventh house. If such combination of Sun and combust Moon is influenced by malefic planets, and/or an overall malefic horoscope, the native may witness various types of problems related to or through his father, mother, marriage and/or children. Considering parents, the native may not have a good equation with his father/mother, his parents may get divorced and he may live with his father/mother, his father/mother may suffer from a long-lasting illness, he/she may be an alcoholic and/or a drug addict, he/she may be a criminal, and/or he/she may die before native's age of 20, depending on native's overall horoscope and running times. He may also witness various types of problems related to properties, vehicles and/or mental health. Considering marriage, the native may witness delay/disturbances in marriage, and/or one or more failed marriages. He may have serious differences of opinion with his wife, she may suffer from a long-lasting illness, she may be an alcoholic and/or a drug addict, she may be a criminal, she may not be loyal to him, she may have extramarital affair/affairs, and/or she may die within 10 or 5 years of marriage. Considering children, the native may lose one or more children through miscarriages that his wife may witness. He may witness delay in childbirth, and/or he may have children who may be physically and/or mentally troubled in some way. He may lose his children through divorce, or his children may engage in immoral/illegal activities.

The native may witness delays, financial losses, setbacks, failures, job loss, bad reputation and several other problems related to or through his profession. Taking an example, suppose combust Moon is placed in the seventh house of a horoscope in Libra with debilitated Sun, Mars, malefic retrograde Mercury and malefic Rahu. Malefic Ketu is placed in the first house in Aries with Jupiter; and Venus is placed in the eighth house in Scorpio with retrograde Saturn. Grahan Yoga is formed in the seventh house whereas Guru Chandal Yoga is formed in the first house.

In this case, native's father as well as mother may die before his age of 20 or 15. He may not find a permanent profession till his age of 35/40, or throughout his life, though he may earn well at times. He may witness setbacks, failures and financial losses through profession. He may witness 1 or 2 failed marriages. He may lose his first wife to death. He may lose one or more children to death, through miscarriages that his wife/wives may witness.

Combust Moon in Seventh House in Scorpio

When Sun and combust Moon are placed in the seventh house of a horoscope in Scorpio, Taurus rises in the ascendant. Sun rules the fourth house, and Moon rules the third house. In general, this combination is benefic here, in most cases. The concept of various planets exhibiting tendencies to be benefic or malefic on the basis of the houses they rule in a horoscope has been explained in the book 'Gemstones: Magic or Science?'.

Combination of Sun and combust Moon in the seventh house of horoscope in Scorpio is benefic in most cases, though it may turn malefic in some cases. It may happen when such combination is influenced by one or more malefic planets, and/or an overall malefic horoscope. The concept of a benefic planet turning malefic due to influences of malefic planets has been explained in the book 'Match Making and Manglik Dosh'.

When benefic in nature, combination of Sun and combust Moon in the seventh house of a horoscope in Scorpio can bless the native with good results related to father, mother, education, wealth, properties, vehicles, siblings, colleagues, marriage, husband, wife, profession, finances, reputation, authority, recognition, fame and several other good results, depending on his/her overall horoscope and running times.

Such combination of Sun and combust Moon can render various types of benefits to the native, related to or through

his father, mother, marriage, and/or siblings. Considering parents, native's father/mother may be a rich man/woman, a celebrity, an officer in government or a powerful politician. The native may enjoy many benefits because of his father/mother's money, influence and/or status. He/she may give a big amount of money, and/or wealth to the native, while he/she's alive, and/or through his/her will. This combination can bless the native with good education, vehicles, residential house/houses and/or several other good results. Considering marriage, the native may witness several benefits due to or through his wife and/or her family members. Considering siblings, some of them may stand by the native and they may help him get out of his problems, many times in his life.

Looking at profession, such combust Moon can help the native achieve success as a fire fighter, fitness trainer, body builder, sportsman, athlete, physician, dietician, lawyer, astrologer, tantric, psychic, spiritual guru, healer, religious guru, teacher, preacher, consultant, researcher, analyst, host, artist, poet, chef, interior designer, police officer, army, air force, naval, revenue, administrative, foreign services officer, judge, doctor, scientist, engineer, politician, professional dealing in education industry, coaching, food, health, pharma, medical, nursing, homecare, real estate, agriculture, hospitality, beauty, fashion, finance, television, music, sports, media, book, publishing, fitness, travel, hotel, airline, fishing, shipping, telecom, computer, software, IT, internet industry or some other type of professional, depending on his/her overall horoscope and running times.

Such combust Moon can help the native achieve success through a creative field as an actor, singer, musician, writer,

dancer, sportsman, artist, architect, designer, developer or some other likewise professional. Taking an example, suppose benefic combust Moon is placed in the seventh house of a horoscope in Scorpio with benefic Sun. Benefic Mercury is placed in the eighth house in Sagittarius with Venus, Mars and Ketu; benefic Rahu is placed in the second house in Gemini, benefic Saturn is placed in the ninth house in Capricorn, and Jupiter is placed in the eleventh house in Pisces.

In this case, the native may write non-fictional books, and he may come across very good amount of success, money, recognition and fame. He may write in the genres of history, war and investigation. He may deliver several bestsellers, and he may receive many awards. If the finer factors and running times are supportive, he may become one of the most successful writers of his time, and his net worth may be in multimillions.

Taking an example for a female native, suppose benefic combust Moon is placed in the seventh house of a horoscope in Scorpio with benefic retrograde Mercury, benefic Sun and benefic debilitated Rahu. Benefic debilitated Ketu is placed in the first house in Taurus, debilitated Mars is placed in the third house in Cancer, Jupiter is placed in the fifth house in Virgo, benefic Saturn is placed in the ninth house in Capricorn, and Venus is placed in the eighth house in Sagittarius.

In this case, the native may become a singer, actor and songwriter. She may possess remarkable talent as a singer, and she may come across very good amount of success, money, recognition and fame. She may deliver several hit songs, and she may receive many awards. She may also perform well as an actor, in the genres of comedy, drama and romance. If the finer factors and running times are supportive, she may become one of the most recognized creative artists of her time, and her net worth may be in billions, by her age of 30/35.

On the other hand, when malefic in nature, combination of Sun and combust Moon in the seventh house of a horoscope in Scorpio can trouble the native with problems related to father, mother, education, wealth, properties, vehicles, siblings, colleagues, marriage, husband, wife, profession, finances, reputation, authority, recognition and several other problems, depending on his/her overall horoscope and running times.

Sun rules the fourth house, Moon rules the third house, and they are placed in the seventh house. If such combination of Sun and combust Moon is influenced by malefic planets, and/or an overall malefic horoscope, the native may witness various types of problems related to or through his father, mother, marriage and/or siblings. Considering parents, the native may not have a good equation with his father/mother, his parents may get divorced and he may live with his father/mother, his father/mother may suffer from a long-lasting illness, he/she may be an alcoholic and/or a drug addict, he/she may be a criminal, and/or he/she may die before native's age of 20, depending on native's overall horoscope and running times. He may also witness various types of problems related to properties, vehicles and/or mental health. Considering marriage, the native may witness delay/disturbances in marriage, and/or one or more failed marriages. He may have serious differences of opinion with his wife, she may suffer from a long-lasting illness, she may be an alcoholic and/or a drug addict, she may be a criminal, she may not be loyal to him, she may have extramarital affair/affairs, and/or she may die within 10 or 5 years of marriage. Considering siblings, the native may have bad relationships with some of his siblings, and/or he may witness various types of problems through them or due to them. The native may have siblings who may be criminals, and/or drug addicts, and he may face several problems because of them. In an extreme case, the native may lose one or more siblings to death, before his age of 40 or 35.

The native may witness delays, financial losses, setbacks, failures, job loss, bad reputation and several other problems related to or through his profession. Taking an example, suppose combust Moon is placed in the seventh house of a horoscope in Scorpio with Sun, Venus and malefic Mars. Malefic Rahu is placed in the sixth house in Libra with malefic retrograde Jupiter; malefic Ketu is placed in the twelfth house in Aries with debilitated Saturn; and Mercury is placed in the eighth house in Sagittarius. Guru Chandal Yoga is formed in the sixth house.

In this case, the native's father as well as mother may die before his age of 20/15. The native may not find a permanent profession throughout his life, and he may keep losing jobs. He may remain jobless for periods of more than 6 months, many times in his life. He may witness several problems because of some of his siblings, and he may lose one or more siblings to death, before his age of 35/30. He may witness 2 or 3 failed marriages. He may lose his first wife to death.

Combust Moon in Seventh House in Sagittarius

When Sun and combust Moon are placed in the seventh house of a horoscope in Sagittarius, Gemini rises in the ascendant. Sun rules the third house, and Moon rules the second house. In general, this combination is benefic here, in most cases. The concept of various planets exhibiting tendencies to be benefic or malefic on the basis of the houses they rule in a horoscope has been explained in the book 'Gemstones: Magic or Science?'.

Combination of Sun and combust Moon in the seventh house of horoscope in Sagittarius is benefic in most cases, though it may turn malefic in some cases. It may happen when such combination is influenced by one or more malefic planets, and/or an overall malefic horoscope. The concept of a benefic planet turning malefic due to influences of malefic planets has been explained in the book 'Match Making and Manglik Dosh'.

When benefic in nature, combination of Sun and combust Moon in the seventh house of a horoscope in Sagittarius can bless the native with good results related to father, mother, family, wealth, speech, siblings, colleagues, marriage, husband, wife, profession, finances, reputation, authority, recognition, fame and several other good results, depending on his/her overall horoscope and running times.

Such combination of Sun and combust Moon can render various types of benefits to the native, related to or through his father, mother, marriage, siblings and/or family. Considering parents, native's father/mother may be a rich man/woman, a celebrity, an officer in government or a powerful politician. The native may enjoy many benefits because of his father/mother's money, influence and/or status. He/she may give a big amount of money, and/or wealth to the native, while he/she's alive, and/or through his/her will. Considering marriage, the native may get married to a woman who may be beautiful, rich, a celebrity, an officer in government, a powerful politician, a successful businesswoman, and/or a citizen of a foreign country. The native may witness several benefits due to or through his wife and/or her family members. Considering siblings, some of them may stand by the native and they may help him get out of his problems, many times in his life.

Looking at profession, such combust Moon can help the native achieve success as a fire fighter, fitness trainer, body builder, sportsman, athlete, physician, dietician, lawyer, astrologer, tantric, psychic, spiritual guru, healer, religious guru, teacher, preacher, consultant, researcher, analyst, host, artist, poet, chef, interior designer, police officer, army, air force, naval, revenue, administrative, foreign services officer, judge, doctor, scientist, engineer, politician, professional dealing in education industry, coaching, food, health, pharma, medical, nursing, homecare, real estate, agriculture, hospitality, beauty, fashion, finance, television, music, sports, media, book, publishing, fitness, travel, hotel, airline, fishing, shipping, telecom, computer, software, IT, internet industry or some other type of professional, depending on his/her overall horoscope and running times.

Such combust Moon can help the native achieve success through a creative field as an actor, singer, musician, writer,

dancer, sportsman, artist, architect, designer, developer or some other likewise professional. Taking an example, suppose benefic combust Moon is placed in the seventh house of a horoscope in Sagittarius with Venus, benefic Sun and benefic Mercury. Benefic Rahu is placed in the second house in Cancer with debilitated Mars; Ketu is placed in the eighth house in Capricorn, benefic retrograde Jupiter is placed in the first house in Gemini, and Saturn is placed in the fourth house in Virgo. Sun and Mercury form Budhaditya Yoga in the seventh house.

In this case, the native may become an actor. He may possess remarkable acting talent, and he may come across very good amount of success, money, recognition and fame. He may perform very well in the genres of action, romance and drama. He may deliver several hit movies, and he may receive many awards. If the finer factors and running times are supportive, he may become one of the most successful actors of his time, and his net worth may be in multimillions.

Taking an example for a female native, suppose benefic combust Moon is placed in the seventh house of a horoscope in Sagittarius with benefic Sun. Benefic retrograde Mercury is placed in the sixth house in Scorpio, Mars is placed in the tenth house in Pisces, benefic Rahu is placed in the eighth house in Capricorn with Venus; Ketu is placed in the second house in Cancer, and retrograde Saturn is placed in the twelfth house in Taurus. In this case, the native may become a tennis player, and she may witness good results.

If benefic Jupiter is placed in the sixth house in Scorpio with Mercury, the equation may become better. The native may possess remarkable talent related to the sport, and she may come across very good amount of success, money, recognition and fame. She may win majority of her matches as well as several championship titles. If the finer factors and running times are supportive, she may become one of the most successful tennis players of her time, she may rank number 1 in the world, and her net worth may be in multimillions.

On the other hand, when malefic in nature, combination of Sun and combust Moon in the seventh house of a horoscope in Sagittarius can trouble the native with problems related to father, mother, family, wealth, speech, siblings, colleagues, marriage, husband, wife, profession, finances, reputation, authority, recognition and several other problems, depending on his/her overall horoscope and running times.

Sun rules the third house, Moon rules the second house, and they are placed in the seventh house. If such combination of Sun and combust Moon is influenced by malefic planets, and/or an overall malefic horoscope, the native may witness various types of problems related to or through his father, mother, marriage, siblings and/or family. Considering parents, the native may not have a good equation with his father/ mother, his parents may get divorced and he may live with his father/mother, his father/mother may suffer from a long-lasting illness, he/she may be an alcoholic and/or a drug addict, he/she may be a criminal, and/or he/she may die before native's age of 20, depending on native's overall horoscope and running times. Considering marriage, the native may witness delay/disturbances in marriage, and/or one or more failed marriages. He may have serious differences of opinion with his wife, she may suffer from a long-lasting illness, she may be an alcoholic and/or a drug addict, she may be a criminal, she may not be loyal to him, she may have extramarital affair/affairs, and/or she may die within 10 or 5 years of marriage. Considering siblings, the native may have bad relationships with some of his siblings, and/or he may witness various types of problems through them or due to them. In an extreme case, the native may lose one or more siblings to death, before his age of 40 or 35.

The native may witness delays, financial losses, setbacks, failures, job loss, bad reputation and several other problems related to or through his profession. Taking an example, suppose combust Moon is placed in the seventh house of a horoscope in Sagittarius with Sun, Venus and malefic Mars. Malefic debilitated Rahu is placed in the sixth house in Scorpio with Mercury; malefic debilitated Ketu and Jupiter form Guru Chandal Yoga in the twelfth house in Taurus, and retrograde Saturn is placed in the fourth house in Virgo.

In this case, native's mother may die before his age of 10 or 5. His father may get married again, but the native may not have a good equation with his stepmother. She may also die before native's age of 20 or 15. The native may not find a permanent profession throughout his life, and he may only find temporary jobs, though he may earn well at times. He may remain jobless for periods of more than 3 months, many times in his life. He may lose one or more siblings to death, before his age of 35/30. He may witness 1 or 2 failed marriages.

Combust Moon in Seventh House in Capricorn

When Sun and combust Moon are placed in the seventh house of a horoscope in Capricorn, Cancer rises in the ascendant. Sun rules the second house, and Moon rules the first house. In general, this combination is benefic here, in most cases. The concept of various planets exhibiting tendencies to be benefic or malefic on the basis of the houses they rule in a horoscope has been explained in the book 'Gemstones: Magic or Science?'.

Combination of Sun and combust Moon in the seventh house of horoscope in Capricorn is benefic in most cases, though it may turn malefic in some cases. It may happen when such combination is influenced by one or more malefic planets, and/or an overall malefic horoscope. The concept of a benefic planet turning malefic due to influences of malefic planets has been explained in the book 'Match Making and Manglik Dosh'.

When benefic in nature, combination of Sun and combust Moon in the seventh house of a horoscope in Capricorn can bless the native with good results related to father, mother, health, lifespan, family, wealth, speech, marriage, husband, wife, profession, finances, reputation, authority, recognition, fame and several other good results, depending on his/her overall horoscope and running times.

Such combination of Sun and combust Moon can render various types of benefits to the native, related to or through his

father, mother, marriage, family and/or lifespan. Considering parents, native's father/mother may be a rich man/woman, a celebrity, an officer in government or a powerful politician. The native may enjoy many benefits because of his father/mother's money, influence and/or status. He/she may give a big amount of money, and/or wealth to the native, while he/she's alive, and/or through his/her will. Considering marriage, the native may get married to a woman who may be beautiful, rich, a celebrity, an officer in government, a powerful politician, a successful businesswoman, and/or a citizen of a foreign country. The native may witness several benefits due to or through his wife and/or her family members. Considering family, the native may be born in a rich, influential, resourceful, well-respected, politically powerful, royal and/or spiritually advanced family, and he may witness several benefits by virtue of being a member of such family. The native may be a good, very good or gifted speaker, and he may achieve good results in many spheres of his life, by virtue of his speech abilities.

Looking at profession, such combust Moon can help the native achieve success as a fire fighter, fitness trainer, body builder, sportsman, athlete, physician, dietician, lawyer, astrologer, tantric, psychic, spiritual guru, healer, religious guru, teacher, preacher, consultant, actor, singer, musician, writer, dancer, sportsman, artist, architect, designer, developer, poet, chef, interior designer, host, researcher, analyst, professional dealing in education industry, coaching, food, health, pharma, medical, nursing, homecare, real estate, agriculture, hospitality, beauty, fashion, finance, television, music, sports, media, book, publishing, fitness, travel, hotel, airline, fishing, shipping, telecom, computer, software, IT, internet industry or some other type of professional, depending on his/her overall horoscope and running times.

Taking an example, suppose benefic combust Moon is placed in the seventh house of a horoscope in Capricorn with Saturn and benefic Sun. Benefic Venus is placed in the sixth house in Sagittarius with Mercury; benefic exalted Rahu is placed in the eleventh house in Taurus, exalted Ketu is placed in the fifth house in Scorpio, and Jupiter is placed in the second house in Leo. In this case, the native may start a bank, and he may witness good results.

If benefic Mars is placed in the ninth house in Pisces, the equation may become better. In this case, the native may come across very good amount of success, money and recognition through banking industry. His business may expand after his age of 40/45, and it may keep growing. If the finer factors and running times are supportive, he may own a large bank having several branches, worth in billions, by his age of 55/60.

Such combust Moon can bless the native with authority in government as a police officer, army, air force, naval, revenue, administrative, foreign services officer, judge, doctor, scientist, engineer, politician or some other type of professional. Taking an example, suppose benefic combust Moon is placed in the seventh house of a horoscope in Capricorn with Saturn, benefic Sun and benefic Venus. Benefic Rahu is placed in the sixth house in Sagittarius with Mercury; Ketu is placed in the twelfth house in Gemini, and retrograde Jupiter is placed in the third house in Virgo. In this case, the native may engage in politics, and he may become a member of parliament of his country.

If benefic debilitated Mars is placed in the first house in Cancer, the equation may become better. In this case, the native may come across very good amount of success, recognition, authority and fame through politics. He may win several elections, and he may become a minister in national government. If the finer factors and running times are supportive, he may serve as prime minister or president of his country.

On the other hand, when malefic in nature, combination of Sun and combust Moon in the seventh house of a horoscope in Capricorn can trouble the native with problems related to father, mother, health, lifespan, family, wealth, speech, marriage, husband, wife, profession, finances, reputation, authority, recognition and several other problems, depending on his/her overall horoscope and running times.

Sun rules the second house, Moon rules the first house, and they are placed in the seventh house. If such combination of Sun and combust Moon is influenced by malefic planets, and/or an overall malefic horoscope, the native may witness various types of problems related to or through his father, mother, marriage, family and/or lifespan. Considering parents, the native may not have a good equation with his father/mother, his parents may get divorced and he may live with his father/mother, his father/mother may suffer from a long-lasting illness, he/she may be an alcoholic and/or a drug addict, he/she may be a criminal, and/or he/she may die before native's age of 20, depending on native's overall horoscope and running times. Considering marriage, the native may witness delay/disturbances in marriage, and/or one or more failed marriages. He may have serious differences of opinion with his wife, she may suffer from a long-lasting illness, she may be an alcoholic and/or a drug addict, she may be a criminal, she may not be loyal to him, she may have extramarital affair/affairs, and/or she may die within 10 or 5 years of marriage. Considering lifespan, the native may witness reduction in lifespan due to several reasons. For example, the native may die in an accident, through a natural disaster, due to a fatal disease, due to a fatal viral infection like COVID, due to drug addiction, he may commit suicide, or someone may kill him

The native may witness delays, financial losses, setbacks, failures, job loss, bad reputation and several other problems related to or through his profession. Taking an example, suppose combust Moon is placed in the seventh house of a horoscope in Capricorn with Sun, malefic Mercury and malefic retrograde Saturn. Malefic debilitated Rahu is placed in the ninth house in Pisces, malefic debilitated Ketu is placed in the third house in Virgo with Mars; and Venus is placed in the sixth house in Sagittarius with Jupiter.

In this case, native's father may die before native's age of 10 or 5. His mother may get married again, but the native may not have a good equation with his stepfather. The native may not find a permanent profession till his age of 35/40, or throughout his life, though he may earn well at times. He may witness financial losses and bad reputation through profession. He may witness 1 or 2 failed marriages, and he may not get married after that. He may die before his age of 50 or 45, due to some type of cancer, another fatal disease, or because of a fatal viral infection like COVID.

Combust Moon in Seventh House in Aquarius

When Sun and combust Moon are placed in the seventh house of a horoscope in Aquarius, Leo rises in the ascendant. Sun rules the first house, and Moon rules the twelfth house. In general, this combination is partly benefic and partly malefic here, though the malefic part is higher, in most cases. The concept of various planets exhibiting tendencies to be benefic or malefic on the basis of the houses they rule in a horoscope has been explained in the book 'Gemstones: Magic or Science?'.

Combination of Sun and combust Moon in the seventh house of horoscope in Aquarius is malefic in many cases, though it may turn benefic in some cases. It may happen when such combination is influenced by one or more benefic planets, and/or an overall benefic horoscope. The concept of a malefic planet turning benefic due to influences of benefic planets has been explained in the book 'Match Making and Manglik Dosh'.

When benefic in nature, combination of Sun and combust Moon in the seventh house of a horoscope in Aquarius can bless the native with good results related to father, mother, health, lifespan, marriage, husband, wife, profession, finances, reputation, authority, recognition, fame and several other good results, depending on his/her overall horoscope and running times.

Such combination of Sun and combust Moon can render various types of benefits to the native, related to or through

his father, mother, marriage and/or lifespan. Considering parents, native's father/mother may be a rich man/woman, a celebrity, an officer in government or a powerful politician. The native may enjoy many benefits because of his father/mother's money, influence and/or status. He/she may give a big amount of money, and/or wealth to the native, while he/she's alive, and/or through his/her will. Considering marriage, the native may get married to a woman who may be beautiful, rich, a celebrity, an officer in government, a powerful politician, a successful businesswoman, and/or a citizen of a foreign country. The native may witness several benefits due to or through his wife and/or her family members.

Looking at profession, such combust Moon can help the native achieve success as a fire fighter, fitness trainer, body builder, sportsman, athlete, physician, dietician, lawyer, astrologer, tantric, psychic, spiritual guru, healer, religious guru, teacher, preacher, consultant, researcher, analyst, host, artist, poet, chef, interior designer, professional dealing in education industry, coaching, food, health, pharma, medical, nursing, homecare, real estate, agriculture, hospitality, beauty, fashion, finance, television, music, sports, media, book, publishing, fitness, travel, hotel, airline, fishing, shipping, telecom, computer, software, IT, internet industry or some other type of professional, depending on his/her overall horoscope and running times.

Such combust Moon can help the native achieve success through a creative field as an actor, singer, musician, writer, dancer, sportsman, artist, architect, designer, developer or some other likewise professional. Taking an example, suppose combust Moon is placed in the seventh house of a horoscope in Aquarius with benefic Sun and benefic Mercury. Benefic Venus is placed in the sixth house in Capricorn with Saturn; benefic exalted Rahu is placed in the second house in Virgo, exalted Ketu is placed in the eighth house in Pisces, and retrograde Jupiter is placed in the eleventh house in Gemini. Sun and Mercury form Budhaditya Yoga in the seventh house. In this case, the native may become a fashion designer, and he may witness good results.

If benefic retrograde Mars is placed in the ninth house in Aries, the equation may become better. The native may start a company which may make various types of fashion products, and he may come across very good amount of success, money, recognition and fame. He may design costumes for several celebrities. His business may expand after his age of 35/40, and it may keep growing. If the finer factors and running times are supportive, he may own a business empire worth in billions, by his age of 55/60.

Such combust Moon can bless the native with authority in government as a police officer, army, air force, naval, revenue, administrative, foreign services officer, judge, doctor, scientist, engineer, politician or some other type of professional. Taking an example, suppose combust Moon is placed in the seventh house of a horoscope in Aquarius with benefic Sun, benefic Venus and benefic Mars. Benefic Mercury is placed in the sixth house in Capricorn, retrograde Jupiter is placed in the second house in Virgo with debilitated Ketu; benefic debilitated Rahu is placed in the eighth house in Pisces, and retrograde Saturn is placed in the eleventh house in Gemini.

In this case, the native may achieve success in civil exams, and he may get selected for the highest possible direct rank in foreign services of his country. He may serve at several important posts during his career, and he may come across very good amount of success, recognition and authority. He may represent his country in several countries of the world. If the finer factors and running times are supportive, he may serve at one of the top 2 ranks in foreign services, before retirement.

On the other hand, when malefic in nature, combination of Sun and combust Moon in the seventh house of a horoscope in Aquarius can trouble the native with problems related to father, mother, health, lifespan, marriage, husband, wife, profession, finances, reputation, authority, recognition and several other problems, depending on his/her overall horoscope and running times.

Sun rules the first house, Moon rules the twelfth house, and they are placed in the seventh house. If such combination of Sun and combust Moon is influenced by malefic planets, and/or an overall malefic horoscope, the native may witness various types of problems related to or through his father, mother, marriage and/or lifespan. Considering parents, the native may not have a good equation with his father/mother, his parents may get divorced and he may live with his father/mother, his father/mother may suffer from a long-lasting illness, he/she may be an alcoholic and/or a drug addict, he/she may be a criminal, and/or he/she may die before native's age of 20, depending on native's overall horoscope and running times. Considering marriage, the native may witness delay/disturbances in marriage, and/or one or more failed marriages. He may have serious differences of opinion with his wife, she may suffer from a long-lasting illness, she may be an alcoholic and/or a drug addict, she may be a criminal, she may not be loyal to him, she may have extramarital affair/ affairs, and/or she may die within 10 or 5 years of marriage. Considering lifespan, the native may witness reduction in lifespan due to several reasons. For example, the native may die in an accident, through a natural disaster, due to a fatal disease, due to a fatal viral infection like COVID, due to drug addiction, he may commit suicide, or someone may kill him intentionally or unintentionally.

The native may witness delays, financial losses, setbacks, failures, job loss, bad reputation and several other problems related to or through his profession. Taking an example, suppose malefic combust Moon is placed in the seventh house of a horoscope in Aquarius with Sun, Venus and malefic Rahu. Malefic Ketu is placed in the first house in Leo, retrograde Jupiter is placed in the sixth house in Capricorn with Mercury; and malefic retrograde Saturn is placed in the eighth house in Pisces with Mars. Grahan Yoga is formed in the seventh house.

In this case, native's father may die before native's age of 10 or 5, and his mother may die before his age of 20 or 15. He may not achieve much professional success throughout his life, and he may keep changing jobs, though he may earn well at times. He may remain jobless for periods of more than 3 months, many times in his life. He may witness 1 or 2 failed marriages. He may die before his age of 55 or 50, in an accident, due to a heart attack, because of a fatal viral infection like COVID, or someone may kill him.

Combust Moon in Seventh House in Pisces

When Sun and combust Moon are placed in the seventh house of a horoscope in Pisces, Virgo rises in the ascendant. Sun rules the twelfth house, and Moon rules the eleventh house. In general, this combination is partly benefic and partly malefic here, though the benefic part is higher, in most cases. The concept of various planets exhibiting tendencies to be benefic or malefic on the basis of the houses they rule in a horoscope has been explained in the book 'Gemstones: Magic or Science?'.

Combination of Sun and combust Moon in the seventh house of horoscope in Pisces is benefic in many cases, though it may turn malefic in some cases. It may happen when such combination is influenced by one or more malefic planets, and/or an overall malefic horoscope. The concept of a benefic planet turning malefic due to influences of malefic planets has been explained in the book 'Match Making and Manglik Dosh'.

When benefic in nature, combination of Sun and combust Moon in the seventh house of a horoscope in Pisces can bless the native with good results related to father, mother, friends, marriage, husband, wife, profession, finances, reputation, authority, recognition, fame and several other good results, depending on his/her overall horoscope and running times.

Such combination of Sun and combust Moon can render various types of benefits to the native, related to or through

his father, mother, marriage and/or friends. Considering parents, native's father/mother may be a rich man/woman, a celebrity, an officer in government or a powerful politician. The native may enjoy many benefits because of his father/mother's money, influence and/or status. He/she may give a big amount of money, and/or wealth to the native, while he/she's alive, and/or through his/her will. Considering marriage, the native may get married to a woman who may be beautiful, rich, a celebrity, an officer in government, a powerful politician, a successful businesswoman, and/or a citizen of a foreign country. The native may witness several benefits due to or through his wife and/or her family members. Considering friends, some of his friends may stand by the native and they may help him get out of his problems, many times in his life.

Looking at profession, such combust Moon can help the native achieve success as a fire fighter, fitness trainer, body builder, sportsman, athlete, physician, dietician, lawyer, astrologer, tantric, psychic, spiritual guru, healer, religious guru, teacher, preacher, consultant, researcher, analyst, host, artist, poet, chef, interior designer, police officer, army, air force, naval, revenue, administrative, foreign services officer, judge, doctor, scientist, engineer, politician, professional dealing in education industry, coaching, food, health, pharma, medical, nursing, homecare, real estate, agriculture, hospitality, beauty, fashion, finance, television, music, sports, media, book, publishing, fitness, travel, hotel, airline, fishing, shipping, telecom, computer, software, IT, internet industry or some other type of professional, depending on his/her overall horoscope and running times.

Such combust Moon can help the native achieve success through a creative field as an actor, singer, musician, writer, dancer, sportsman, artist, architect, designer, developer or some other likewise professional. Taking an example, suppose benefic combust Moon is placed in the seventh house of a horoscope in Pisces with Sun, benefic debilitated Mercury and benefic exalted Venus. Exalted Saturn is placed in the second house in Libra, benefic Jupiter is placed in the ninth house in Taurus, benefic Rahu is placed in the eleventh house in Cancer, Ketu is placed in the fifth house in Capricorn, and Mars is placed in the sixth house in Aquarius. Venus forms Malavya Yoga in the seventh house whereas Mercury and Venus form Neechbhang Rajyoga in the same house.

In this case, the native may become a music composer. He may possess remarkable talent, and he may come across very good amount of success, money, recognition and fame. He may compose music for several hit songs, and he may receive many awards. If the finer factors and running times are supportive, he may become one of the most successful music composers of his time, and his net worth may be in multimillions.

Taking another example, suppose benefic combust Moon is placed in the seventh house of a horoscope in Pisces with Sun and benefic debilitated Mercury. Benefic retrograde Venus is placed in the ninth house in Taurus with Mars; benefic Rahu is placed in the fifth house in Capricorn, Ketu is placed in the eleventh house in Cancer, and Saturn is placed in the tenth house in Gemini. In this case, the native may write fictional books, and he may witness good results.

If benefic Jupiter is placed in the third house in Scorpio, the equation may become better. The native may possess remarkable writing talent, and he may come across very good amount of success, money, recognition and fame. He may write in several genres, including mystery, fantasy and thriller. He may deliver several bestsellers, and he may receive many awards. If the finer factors and running times are supportive, he may become one of the most successful writers of his time, and his net worth may be in multimillions.

On the other hand, when malefic in nature, combination of Sun and combust Moon in the seventh house of a horoscope in Pisces can trouble the native with problems related to father, mother, friends, marriage, husband, wife, profession, finances, reputation, authority, recognition and several other problems, depending on his/her overall horoscope and running times.

Sun rules the twelfth house, Moon rules the eleventh house, and they are placed in the seventh house. If such combination of Sun and combust Moon is influenced by malefic planets, and/or an overall malefic horoscope, the native may witness various types of problems related to or through his father, mother, marriage and/or friends. Considering parents, the native may not have a good equation with his father/mother, his parents may get divorced and he may live with his father/ mother, his father/mother may suffer from a long-lasting illness, he/she may be an alcoholic and/or a drug addict, he/ she may be a criminal, and/or he/she may die before native's age of 20, depending on native's overall horoscope and running times. Considering marriage, the native may witness delay/disturbances in marriage, and/or one or more failed marriages. He may have serious differences of opinion with his wife, she may suffer from a long-lasting illness, she may be an alcoholic and/or a drug addict, she may be a criminal, she may not be loyal to him, she may have extramarital affair/affairs, and/or she may die within 10 or 5 years of marriage. Considering friends, some of his friends may be selfish, opportunists, criminal-minded, criminals, drug addicts, traitors and/or they may have some other negative traits. The native may witness several problems because of such friends, many times in his life. In an extreme case, one or more of his good friends may die before native's age of 40 or 35.

The native may witness delays, financial losses, setbacks, failures, job loss, bad reputation and several other problems related to or through his profession. Taking an example, suppose combust Moon is placed in the seventh house of a horoscope in Pisces with malefic Sun. Malefic Mars is placed in the eighth house in Aries with Venus; malefic Rahu is placed in the sixth house in Aquarius with Mercury; malefic Ketu is placed in the twelfth house in Leo with Jupiter; and Saturn is placed in the ninth house in Taurus. Guru Chandal Yoga is formed in the twelfth house.

In this case, the native's mother may die before native's age of 10 or 5. He may not have a good equation with his father. The native may not achieve much professional success till his age of 35/40, or throughout his life, though he may earn well at times. He may remain jobless for periods of more than 3 months, many times in his life. He may lose one or more good friends to death, before his age of 35 or 30. He may witness 1 or 2 failed marriages. He may lose his first wife to death.

Combust Moon in Eighth House in Aries

When Sun and combust Moon are placed in the eighth house of a horoscope in Aries, Virgo rises in the ascendant. Sun rules the twelfth house, and Moon rules the eleventh house. In general, this combination is partly benefic and partly malefic here, though the malefic part is higher, in most cases. The concept of various planets exhibiting tendencies to be benefic or malefic on the basis of the houses they rule in a horoscope has been explained in the book 'Gemstones: Magic or Science?'.

Combination of Sun and combust Moon in the eighth house of horoscope in Aries is malefic in many cases, though it may turn benefic in some cases. It may happen when such combination is influenced by one or more benefic planets, and/or an overall benefic horoscope. The concept of a malefic planet turning benefic due to influences of benefic planets has been explained in the book 'Match Making and Manglik Dosh'.

When benefic in nature, combination of Sun and combust Moon in the eighth house of a horoscope in Aries can bless the native with good results related to father, mother, friends, creativity, spiritual growth, profession, finances, reputation, authority, recognition, fame and several other good results, depending on his/her overall horoscope and running times.

Such combination of Sun and combust Moon can render various types of benefits to the native, related to or through

his father, mother and/or friends. Considering parents, native's father/mother may be a rich man/woman, a celebrity, an officer in government or a powerful politician. The native may enjoy many benefits because of his father/mother's money, influence and/or status. He/she may give a big amount of money, and/or wealth to the native, while he/she's alive, and/or through his/her will. Considering friends, some of his friends may stand by the native and they may help him get out of his problems, many times in his life.

Looking at profession, such combust Moon can help the native achieve success as a fire fighter, fitness trainer, body builder, sportsman, athlete, physician, dietician, lawyer, astrologer, tantric, psychic, spiritual guru, healer, religious guru, teacher, preacher, consultant, actor, singer, musician, writer, dancer, sportsman, artist, architect, designer, developer, poet, chef, interior designer, host, researcher, analyst, professional dealing in education industry, coaching, food, health, pharma, medical, nursing, homecare, real estate, agriculture, hospitality, beauty, fashion, finance, television, music, sports, media, book, publishing, fitness, travel, hotel, airline, fishing, shipping, telecom, computer, software, IT, internet industry or some other type of professional, depending on his/her overall horoscope and running times.

Taking an example, suppose benefic combust Moon is placed in the eighth house of a horoscope in Aries with exalted Sun and benefic Mercury. Benefic Venus is placed in the sixth house in Aquarius with benefic Rahu; Mars is placed in the twelfth house in Leo with Ketu; and Saturn is placed in the fourth house in Sagittarius. In this case, the native may become a scientist, and he may enjoy a good career.

If benefic Jupiter is placed in the third house in Scorpio, the equation may become better. The native may specialize in space science. He may possess remarkable knowledge of his field, and he may come across very good amount of success and recognition, along with good amount of money and authority. He may conduct research, and he may come across discoveries. He may receive awards as well as financial rewards. If the finer factors and running times are supportive, he may have a very successful career, and he may serve as the head of his department for several years.

Such combust Moon can bless the native with authority in government as a police officer, army, air force, naval, revenue, administrative, foreign services officer, judge, doctor, scientist, engineer, politician or some other type of professional. Taking an example, suppose benefic combust Moon is placed in the eighth house of a horoscope in Aries with exalted Sun. Benefic exalted Venus is placed in the seventh house in Pisces with Saturn and benefic debilitated Mercury; benefic Mars is placed in the sixth house in Aquarius, benefic Rahu is placed in the fifth house in Capricorn, and Ketu is placed in the eleventh house in Cancer. Venus forms Malavya Yoga in the seventh house whereas Mercury and Venus form Neechbhang Rajyoga in the same house. In this case, the native may become an officer in army, and he may enjoy a good career.

If benefic Jupiter is placed in the first house in Virgo, the equation may become better. In this case, the native may achieve success in competitive exams, and he may get selected for the highest possible direct rank in army. He may serve at several important posts during his career, and he may come across very good amount of success, recognition and authority.

If the finer factors and running times are supportive, he may serve as the chief of army of his country, before retirement.

On the other hand, when malefic in nature, combination of Sun and combust Moon in the eighth house of a horoscope in Aries can trouble the native with problems related to father, mother, friends, lifespan, profession, finances, reputation, authority, recognition and several other problems, depending on his/her overall horoscope and running times.

Sun rules the twelfth house, Moon rules the eleventh house, and they are placed in the eighth house. If such combination of Sun and combust Moon is influenced by malefic planets, and/or an overall malefic horoscope, the native may witness various types of problems related to or through his father, mother, lifespan and/or friends. Considering parents, the native may not have a good equation with his father/mother, his parents may get divorced and he may live with his father/mother, his father/mother may suffer from a long-lasting illness, he/she may be an alcoholic and/or a drug addict, he/she may be a criminal, and/or he/she may die before native's age of 20, depending on native's overall horoscope and running times. The native may not know his biological father/mother, or his father/mother may refuse to accept him as his/her son, as native may be born from a secret love affair of his father/mother, and he/she may give him to someone else or to an orphanage. In an extreme case, the native may kill his father/mother for some reason, or his father/mother may kill him, depending on native's overall horoscope and running times. Considering friends, some of his friends may be selfish, opportunists, criminal-minded, criminals, drug addicts, traitors and/or they may have some other negative traits. The native may witness several problems because of such friends, many times in his life. In an extreme case, one or more of his good friends may die before native's age of 40 or 35. Considering lifespan, the native may witness reduction in lifespan due to several reasons.

The native may witness delays, financial losses, setbacks, failures, job loss, bad reputation and several other problems related to or through his profession. Taking an example, suppose combust Moon is placed in the eighth house of a horoscope in Aries with retrograde Mercury and malefic exalted Sun. Malefic Mars is placed in the sixth house in Aquarius malefic Ketu; malefic Rahu is placed in the twelfth house in Leo with Jupiter; benefic exalted Venus is placed in the seventh house in Pisces, and Saturn is placed in the tenth house in Gemini. Guru Chandal Yoga is formed in the twelfth house.

In this case, native's father as well as mother may die before his age of 15 or 10. He may not achieve much professional success till his age of 35/40 or throughout his life, though he may earn well at times. He may remain jobless for periods of more than 3 months, many times in his life. He may lose more than one good friend to death, before his age of 35/30. He may witness 1 or 2 failed marriages. He may die before his age of 50 or 45, in an accident, because of a fatal viral infection like COVID, someone may kill him, or he may commit suicide.

Combust Moon in Eighth House in Taurus

When Sun and combust Moon are placed in the eighth house of a horoscope in Taurus, Libra rises in the ascendant. Sun rules the eleventh house, and Moon rules the tenth house. In general, this combination is benefic here, in many cases. The concept of various planets exhibiting tendencies to be benefic or malefic on the basis of the houses they rule in a horoscope has been explained in the book 'Gemstones: Magic or Science?'.

Combination of Sun and combust Moon in the eighth house of horoscope in Taurus is benefic in many cases, though it may turn malefic in some cases. It may happen when such combination is influenced by one or more malefic planets, and/or an overall malefic horoscope. The concept of a benefic planet turning malefic due to influences of malefic planets has been explained in the book 'Match Making and Manglik Dosh'.

When benefic in nature, combination of Sun and combust Moon in the eighth house of a horoscope in Taurus can bless the native with good results related to father, mother, friends, profession, finances, reputation, authority, recognition, fame and several other good results, depending on his/her overall horoscope and running times.

Such combination of Sun and combust Moon can render various types of benefits to the native, related to or through his father, mother and/or friends. Considering parents, native's

father/mother may be a rich man/woman, a celebrity, an officer in government or a powerful politician. The native may enjoy many benefits because of his father/mother's money, influence and/or status. He/she may give a big amount of money, and/or wealth to the native, while he/she's alive, and/ or through his/her will. Considering friends, some of his friends may stand by the native and they may help him get out of his problems, many times in his life. One or more of his friends may help him financially as well as in other ways, in order for him to start a new business, or repair/consolidate an already existing business.

Looking at profession, such combust Moon can help the native achieve success as a fire fighter, fitness trainer, body builder, sportsman, athlete, physician, dietician, lawyer, astrologer, tantric, psychic, spiritual guru, healer, religious guru, teacher, preacher, consultant, actor, singer, musician, writer, dancer, sportsman, artist, architect, designer, developer, poet, chef, interior designer, host, researcher, analyst, professional dealing in education industry, coaching, food, health, pharma, medical, nursing, homecare, real estate, agriculture, hospitality, beauty, fashion, finance, television, music, sports, media, book, publishing, fitness, travel, hotel, airline, fishing, shipping, telecom, computer, software, IT, internet industry or some other type of professional, depending on his/her overall horoscope and running times.

Taking an example, suppose benefic combust Moon is placed in the eighth house of a horoscope in Taurus with Venus, benefic Saturn and benefic Sun. Mercury is placed in the seventh house in Aries, benefic Rahu is placed in the eleventh house in Leo, Ketu is placed in the fifth house in

Aquarius, and retrograde Jupiter is placed in the second house in Scorpio. In this case, the native may start a company which may manufacture cars and other automobiles. He may witness good results.

If benefic Mars is placed in the third house in Sagittarius, the equation may become better. In this case, the native may come across very good amount of success, money and recognition through automobile industry. His business may expand after his age of 35/40, and it may keep growing. If the finer factors and running times are supportive, he may own a business empire worth in billions, by his age of 55/60.

Such combust Moon can bless the native with authority in government as a police officer, army, air force, naval, revenue, administrative, foreign services officer, judge, doctor, scientist, engineer, politician or some other type of professional. Taking an example, suppose benefic combust Moon is placed in the eighth house of a horoscope in Taurus with Venus, Mercury and benefic Sun. Benefic Rahu is placed in the tenth house in Cancer, Ketu is placed in the fourth house in Capricorn, retrograde Jupiter is placed in the ninth house in Gemini, and benefic Mars is placed in the sixth house in Pisces. In this case, the native may become an officer in revenue services, and he may enjoy a good career.

If benefic Saturn is placed in the fourth house in Capricorn with Ketu; the equation may become better. Saturn forms Shasha Yoga in the fourth house. In this case, the native may achieve success in civil exams, and he may get selected for the highest possible direct rank in revenue services. He may serve at several important posts during his career, and he may come across very good amount of success, recognition and authority.

If the finer factors and running times are supportive, he may serve as the head of a revenue department, before retirement.

On the other hand, when malefic in nature, combination of Sun and combust Moon in the eighth house of a horoscope in Taurus can trouble the native with problems related to father, mother, friends, lifespan, profession, finances, reputation, authority, recognition and several other problems, depending on his/her overall horoscope and running times.

Sun rules the eleventh house, Moon rules the tenth house, and they are placed in the eighth house. If such combination of Sun and combust Moon is influenced by malefic planets, and/or an overall malefic horoscope, the native may witness various types of problems related to or through his father, mother, lifespan and/or friends. Considering parents, the native may not have a good equation with his father/mother, his parents may get divorced and he may live with his father/mother, his father/mother may suffer from a long-lasting illness, he/she may be an alcoholic and/or a drug addict, he/she may be a criminal, and/or he/she may die before native's age of 20, depending on native's overall horoscope and running times. The native may not know his biological father/mother, or his father/mother may refuse to accept him as his/her son, as native may be born from a secret love affair of his father/mother, and he/she may give him to someone else or to an orphanage. In an extreme case, the native may kill his father/mother for some reason, or his father/mother may kill him, depending on native's overall horoscope and running times. Considering friends, some of his friends may be selfish, opportunists, criminal-minded, criminals, drug addicts, traitors and/or they may have some other negative traits. The native may witness several problems because of such friends, many times in his life. In an extreme case, one or more of his good friends may die before native's age of 40 or 35. Considering lifespan, the native may witness reduction in lifespan due to several reasons. For example, the native may die in an accident, through a natural disaster, due to a fatal disease, due to a fatal viral infection like COVID, due to drug addiction, he may commit suicide, or someone may kill him intentionally or unintentionally.

The native may witness delays, financial losses, setbacks, failures, job loss, bad reputation and several other problems related to or through his profession. Taking an example, suppose combust Moon is placed in the eighth house of a horoscope in Taurus with Sun, Venus, malefic retrograde Jupiter and malefic debilitated Ketu. Malefic debilitated Rahu is placed in the second house in Scorpio, Saturn is placed in the twelfth house in Virgo, and benefic Mars is placed in the seventh house in Aries with Mercury. Grahan Yoga and Guru Chandal Yoga are formed in the eighth house.

In this case, native's mother may die before his age of 10 or 5, and his father may die before native's age of 20 or 15. The native may not find a permanent profession throughout his life, and he may only find temporary jobs. He may remain jobless for periods of more than 3 months, many times in his life. He may lose one or more good friends to death, before his age of 35 or 30. He may die before his age of 55 or 50, due to a heart attack, some type of cancer, another fatal disease or because of a fatal viral infection like COVID.

Combust Moon in Eighth House in Gemini

When Sun and combust Moon are placed in the eighth house of a horoscope in Gemini, Scorpio rises in the ascendant. Sun rules the tenth house, and Moon rules the ninth house. In general, this combination is benefic here, in many cases. The concept of various planets exhibiting tendencies to be benefic or malefic on the basis of the houses they rule in a horoscope has been explained in the book 'Gemstones: Magic or Science?'.

Combination of Sun and combust Moon in the eighth house of horoscope in Gemini is benefic in many cases, though it may turn malefic in some cases. It may happen when such combination is influenced by one or more malefic planets, and/or an overall malefic horoscope. The concept of a benefic planet turning malefic due to influences of malefic planets has been explained in the book 'Match Making and Manglik Dosh'.

When benefic in nature, combination of Sun and combust Moon in the eighth house of a horoscope in Gemini can bless the native with good results related to father, mother, creativity, spiritual growth, profession, finances, reputation, authority, recognition, fame and several other good results, depending on his/her overall horoscope and running times.

Such combination of Sun and combust Moon can render various types of benefits to the native, related to or through his father and/or mother. Considering parents, native's father/mother may be a rich man/woman, a celebrity, an officer in government or a powerful politician. The native may enjoy many benefits because of his father/mother's money, influence and/or status. He/she may give a big amount of money, and/or wealth to the native, while he/she's alive, and/ or through his/her will.

Looking at profession, such combust Moon can help the native achieve success as a fire fighter, fitness trainer, body builder, sportsman, athlete, physician, dietician, lawyer, astrologer, tantric, psychic, spiritual guru, healer, religious guru, teacher, preacher, consultant, researcher, analyst, host, artist, poet, chef, interior designer, professional dealing in education industry, coaching, food, health, pharma, medical, nursing, homecare, real estate, agriculture, hospitality, beauty, fashion, finance, television, music, sports, media, book, publishing, fitness, travel, hotel, airline, fishing, shipping, telecom, computer, software, IT, internet industry or some other type of professional, depending on his/her overall horoscope and running times.

Such combust Moon can help the native achieve success through a creative field as an actor, singer, musician, writer, dancer, sportsman, artist, architect, designer, developer or some other likewise professional. Taking an example, suppose benefic combust Moon is placed in the eighth house of a horoscope in Gemini with Mercury and benefic Sun. Benefic Jupiter is placed in the eleventh house in Virgo, Mars is placed in the tenth house in Leo, Venus is placed in the sixth house in Aries, benefic debilitated Rahu is placed in the first house in Scorpio, and debilitated Ketu is placed in the seventh house in Taurus. In this case, the native may become a singer, and he may witness good results.

If benefic retrograde Saturn forms Shasha Yoga in the fourth house in Aquarius, the equation may become better. In this case, the native may possess remarkable singing talent, and he may come across very good amount of success, money, recognition and fame. He may deliver several hit songs, and he may receive many awards. If the finer factors and running times are supportive, he may become one of the most recognized singers of his time, and his net worth may be in multimillions.

Such combust Moon can bless the native with authority in government as a police officer, army, air force, naval, revenue, administrative, foreign services officer, judge, doctor, scientist, engineer, politician or some other type of professional. Taking an example, suppose benefic combust Moon is placed in the eighth house of a horoscope in Gemini with Mercury and benefic Sun. Benefic debilitated Rahu is placed in the first house in Scorpio, Venus is placed in the seventh house in Taurus with debilitated Ketu; retrograde Mars is placed in the tenth house in Leo, and benefic exalted Jupiter is placed in the ninth house in Cancer. In this case, the native may become an officer in administrative services, and he may enjoy a good career.

If benefic Saturn forms Shasha Yoga in the fourth house in Aquarius, the equation may become better. In this case, the native may achieve success in civil exams, and he may get selected for the highest possible direct rank in administrative services. He may serve at several important posts during his career, and he may come across very good amount of success, recognition and authority. If the finer factors and running times are supportive, he may serve as the head of an administrative department, before retirement.

On the other hand, when malefic in nature, combination of Sun and combust Moon in the eighth house of a horoscope in Gemini can trouble the native with problems related to father, mother, lifespan, profession, finances, reputation, authority, recognition and several other problems, depending on his/her overall horoscope and running times.

Sun rules the tenth house, Moon rules the ninth house, and they are placed in the eighth house. If such combination of Sun and combust Moon is influenced by malefic planets, and/or an overall malefic horoscope, the native may witness various types of problems related to or through his father, mother and/or lifespan. Considering parents, the native may not have a good equation with his father/mother, his parents may get divorced and he may live with his father/mother, his father/mother may suffer from a long-lasting illness, he/she may be an alcoholic and/or a drug addict, he/she may be a criminal, and/or he/she may die before native's age of 20, depending on native's overall horoscope and running times. The native may not know his biological father/mother, or his father/mother may refuse to accept him as his/her son, as native may be born from a secret love affair of his father/mother, and he/she may give him to someone else or to an orphanage. In an extreme case, the native may kill his father/mother for some reason, or his father/mother may kill him, depending on native's overall horoscope and running times. Considering lifespan, the native may witness reduction in lifespan due to several reasons. For example, the native may die in an accident, through a natural disaster, due to a fatal disease, due to a fatal viral infection like COVID, due to drug addiction, he may commit suicide, or someone may kill him intentionally or unintentionally.

The native may witness delays, financial losses, setbacks, failures, job loss, bad reputation and several other problems related to or through his profession. Taking an example, suppose combust Moon is placed in the eighth house of a horoscope in Gemini with Sun and malefic Mercury. Malefic Venus is placed in the seventh house in Taurus with malefic exalted Rahu; malefic exalted Ketu is placed in the first house in Scorpio with Mars; Jupiter is placed in the twelfth house in Libra, and debilitated Saturn is placed in the sixth house in Aries.

In this case, native's mother may die before his age of 10 or 5, and his father may die before native's age of 20 or 15. The native may not find a permanent profession throughout his life, and he may keep losing jobs, though he may earn well at times. He may remain jobless for periods of more than 3 months, many times in his life. He may witness 1 or 2 failed marriages. He may die before his age of 60 or 55, in an accident, due to a heart attack, because of a fatal viral infection like COVID, or someone may kill him.

Combust Moon in Eighth House in Cancer

When Sun and combust Moon are placed in the eighth house of a horoscope in Cancer, Sagittarius rises in the ascendant. Sun rules the ninth house, and Moon rules the eighth house. In general, this combination is partly benefic and partly malefic here, though the malefic part is higher, in most cases. The concept of various planets exhibiting tendencies to be benefic or malefic on the basis of the houses they rule in a horoscope has been explained in the book 'Gemstones: Magic or Science?'.

Combination of Sun and combust Moon in the eighth house of horoscope in Cancer is malefic in many cases, though it may turn benefic in some cases. It may happen when such combination is influenced by one or more benefic planets, and/or an overall benefic horoscope. The concept of a malefic planet turning benefic due to influences of benefic planets has been explained in the book 'Match Making and Manglik Dosh'.

When benefic in nature, combination of Sun and combust Moon in the eighth house of a horoscope in Cancer can bless the native with good results related to father, mother, creativity, spiritual growth, profession, finances, reputation, authority, recognition, fame and several other good results, depending on his/her overall horoscope and running times.

Such combination of Sun and combust Moon can render various types of benefits to the native, related to or through his father, mother and/or lifespan. Considering parents, native's father/mother may be a rich man/woman, a celebrity, an officer in government or a powerful politician. The native may enjoy many benefits because of his father/mother's money, influence and/or status. He/she may give a big amount of money, and/or wealth to the native, while he/she's alive, and/or through his/her will.

Looking at profession, such combust Moon can help the native achieve success as a fire fighter, fitness trainer, body builder, sportsman, athlete, physician, dietician, lawyer, astrologer, tantric, psychic, spiritual guru, healer, religious guru, teacher, preacher, consultant, researcher, analyst, host, artist, poet, chef, interior designer, professional dealing in education industry, coaching, food, health, pharma, medical, nursing, homecare, real estate, agriculture, hospitality, beauty, fashion, finance, television, music, sports, media, book, publishing, fitness, travel, hotel, airline, fishing, shipping, telecom, computer, software, IT, internet industry or some other type of professional, depending on his/her overall horoscope and running times.

Such combust Moon can help the native achieve success through a creative field as an actor, singer, musician, writer, dancer, sportsman, artist, architect, designer, developer or some other likewise professional. Taking an example, suppose combust Moon is placed in the eighth house of a horoscope in Cancer with debilitated Mars and benefic Sun. Benefic retrograde Jupiter is placed in the third house in Aquarius, benefic Saturn is placed in the fourth house in Pisces, Venus is placed in the ninth house in Leo, benefic debilitated Rahu is placed in the twelfth house in Scorpio, and debilitated Ketu is placed in the sixth house in Taurus. In this case, the native may become a comic book writer, and he may witness good results.

If benefic Mercury is placed in the ninth house in Leo with Venus, the equation may become better. The native may possess remarkable talent, and he may come across very good amount of success, money, recognition and fame as a comic book writer. He may deliver several bestselling comics, and some of them may be converted into movies. If the finer factors and running times are supportive, he may become one of the most successful comic book writers of his time, and his net worth may be in multimillions.

Such combust Moon can bless the native with authority in government as a police officer, army, air force, naval, revenue, administrative, foreign services officer, judge, doctor, scientist, engineer, politician or some other type of professional. Taking an example, suppose combust Moon is placed in the eighth house of a horoscope in Cancer with Venus, benefic Sun and benefic Mercury. Benefic exalted Rahu is placed in the tenth house in Virgo, exalted Ketu is placed in the fourth house in Pisces, Mars is placed in the sixth house in Taurus, and benefic retrograde Jupiter is placed in the ninth house in Leo. In this case, the native may engage in politics, and he may become a member of parliament of his country.

If benefic Saturn is placed in the first house in Sagittarius, the equation may become better. In this case, the native may come across very good amount of success, recognition, authority and fame through politics. He may win several elections, and he may become a minister in national government. If the finer factors and running times are supportive, he may serve as prime minister or president of his country.

On the other hand, when malefic in nature, combination of Sun and combust Moon in the eighth house of a horoscope in Cancer can trouble the native with problems related to father, mother, lifespan, profession, finances, reputation, authority, recognition and several other problems, depending on his/her overall horoscope and running times.

Sun rules the ninth house, Moon rules the eighth house, and they are placed in the eighth house. If such combination of Sun and combust Moon is influenced by malefic planets, and/or an overall malefic horoscope, the native may witness various types of problems related to or through his father, mother and/or lifespan. Considering parents, the native may not have a good equation with his father/mother, his parents may get divorced and he may live with his father/mother, his father/mother may suffer from a long-lasting illness, he/she may be an alcoholic and/or a drug addict, he/she may be a criminal, and/or he/she may die before native's age of 20, depending on native's overall horoscope and running times. The native may not know his biological father/mother, or his father/mother may refuse to accept him as his/her son, as native may be born from a secret love affair of his father/mother, and he/she may give him to someone else or to an orphanage. In an extreme case, the native may kill his father/mother for some reason, or his father/mother may kill him, depending on native's overall horoscope and running times. Considering lifespan, the native may witness reduction in lifespan due to several reasons. For example, the native may die in an accident, through a natural disaster, due to a fatal disease, due to a fatal viral infection like COVID, due to drug addiction, he may commit suicide, or someone may kill him intentionally or unintentionally.

The native may witness delays, financial losses, setbacks, failures, job loss, bad reputation and several other problems related to or through his profession. Taking an example, suppose malefic combust Moon is placed in the eighth house of a horoscope in Cancer with Sun, debilitated Mars and malefic Rahu. Malefic Ketu is placed in the second house in Capricorn with retrograde Saturn; malefic retrograde Venus is placed in the ninth house in Leo with retrograde Mercury; and Jupiter is placed in the twelfth house in Scorpio. Grahan Yoga and Angarak Yoga are formed in the eighth house.

In this case, native's father may die before his age of 10 or 5. His mother may get married again, but the native may not have a good equation with his stepfather. Native's mother may also die before native's age of 20 or 15. He may not achieve much professional success till his age of 35/40, or throughout his life, though he may earn well at times. He may witness financial losses and bad reputation through profession. He may witness 1 or 2 failed marriages. He may die before his age of 60 or 55, due to a heart attack, some type of cancer, another fatal disease, or because of a fatal viral infection like COVID.

Combust Moon in Eighth House in Leo

When Sun and combust Moon are placed in the eighth house of a horoscope in Leo, Capricorn rises in the ascendant. Sun rules the eighth house, and Moon rules the seventh house. In general, this combination is partly benefic and partly malefic here, though the malefic part is higher, in most cases. The concept of various planets exhibiting tendencies to be benefic or malefic on the basis of the houses they rule in a horoscope has been explained in the book 'Gemstones: Magic or Science?'.

Combination of Sun and combust Moon in the eighth house of horoscope in Leo is malefic in many cases, though it may turn benefic in some cases. It may happen when such combination is influenced by one or more benefic planets, and/or an overall benefic horoscope. The concept of a malefic planet turning benefic due to influences of benefic planets has been explained in the book 'Match Making and Manglik Dosh'.

When benefic in nature, combination of Sun and combust Moon in the eighth house of a horoscope in Leo can bless the native with good results related to father, mother, marriage, husband, wife, profession, finances, reputation, authority, recognition, fame and several other good results, depending on his/her overall horoscope and running times.

Such combination of Sun and combust Moon can render various types of benefits to the native, related to or through his father, mother and/or marriage. Considering parents, native's

father/mother may be a rich man/woman, a celebrity, an officer in government or a powerful politician. The native may enjoy many benefits because of his father/mother's money, influence and/or status. He/she may give a big amount of money, and/or wealth to the native, while he/she's alive, and/ or through his/her will. Considering marriage, the native may get married to a woman who may be beautiful, rich, a celebrity, an officer in government, a powerful politician, a successful businesswoman, and/or a citizen of a foreign country. The native may witness several benefits due to or through his wife and/or her family members.

Looking at profession, such combust Moon can help the native achieve success as a fire fighter, fitness trainer, body builder, sportsman, athlete, physician, dietician, lawyer, astrologer, tantric, psychic, spiritual guru, healer, religious guru, teacher, preacher, consultant, actor, singer, musician, writer, dancer, sportsman, artist, architect, designer, developer, poet, chef, interior designer, host, researcher, analyst, professional dealing in education industry, coaching, food, health, pharma, medical, nursing, homecare, real estate, agriculture, hospitality, beauty, fashion, finance, television, music, sports, media, book, publishing, fitness, travel, hotel, airline, fishing, shipping, telecom, computer, software, IT, internet industry or some other type of professional, depending on his/her overall horoscope and running times.

Taking an example, suppose benefic combust Moon is placed in the eighth house of a horoscope in Leo with Sun and Mercury. Benefic Venus is placed in the seventh house in Cancer with benefic Saturn; retrograde Jupiter is placed in the sixth house in Gemini with benefic Rahu; Ketu is placed in the twelfth house in Sagittarius, and benefic Mars is placed in the ninth house in Virgo.

In this case, the native may become a doctor. He may specialize in cardiology. He may possess remarkable knowledge of his field, and he may come across very good amount of success, money and recognition. He may start his own hospital after his age of 35/40, and he may witness very good results. If the finer factors and running times are supportive, he may become one of the most successful cardiologists of his region, and his net worth may be in multimillions.

Such combust Moon can bless the native with authority in government as a police officer, army, air force, naval, revenue, administrative, foreign services officer, judge, doctor, scientist, engineer, politician or some other type of professional. Taking an example, suppose benefic combust Moon is placed in the eighth house of a horoscope in Leo with Sun and benefic Rahu. Ketu is placed in the second house in Aquarius, benefic Venus is placed in the seventh house in Cancer, benefic Mars is placed in the ninth house in Virgo with exalted Mercury; and benefic retrograde Saturn is placed in the first house in Capricorn with retrograde Jupiter. Saturn forms Shasha Yoga in the first house.

In this case, the native may achieve success in civil exams, and he may get selected for the highest possible direct rank in police force. He may serve at several important posts during his career, and he may come across very good amount of success, recognition and authority. If the finer factors and running times are supportive, he may serve as the chief of police of a state, before retirement.

On the other hand, when malefic in nature, combination of Sun and combust Moon in the eighth house of a horoscope in Leo can trouble the native with problems related to father, mother, marriage, husband, wife, lifespan, profession, finances, reputation, authority, recognition and several other problems, depending on his/her overall horoscope and running times.

Sun rules the eighth house, Moon rules the seventh house, and they are placed in the eighth house. If such combination of Sun and combust Moon is influenced by malefic planets, and/or an overall malefic horoscope, the native may witness various types of problems related to or through his father, mother, lifespan and/or marriage. Considering parents, the native may not have a good equation with his father/mother, his parents may get divorced and he may live with his father/mother, his father/mother may suffer from a long-lasting illness, he/she may be an alcoholic and/or a drug addict, he/she may be a criminal, and/or he/she may die before native's age of 20, depending on native's overall horoscope and running times. The native may not know his biological father/mother, or his father/mother may refuse to accept him as his/her son, as native may be born from a secret love affair of his father/mother, and he/she may give him to someone else or to an orphanage. In an extreme case, the native may kill his father/mother for some reason, or his father/mother may kill him, depending on native's overall horoscope and running times. Considering marriage, the native may witness delay/disturbances in marriage, and/or one or more failed marriages. He may have serious differences of opinion with his wife, she may suffer from a long-lasting illness, she may be an alcoholic and/or a drug addict, she may be a criminal, she may not be loyal to him, she may have extramarital affair/affairs, and/or she may die within 10 or 5 years of marriage. In an extreme case, she may kill the native due to some reason, or the native may kill her, depending on native's overall horoscope and running times. Considering lifespan, the native may witness reduction in lifespan due to several reasons.

The native may witness delays, financial losses, setbacks, failures, job loss, bad reputation and several other problems related to or through his profession. Taking an example, suppose combust Moon is placed in the eighth house of a horoscope in Leo with malefic Sun. Mercury is placed in the seventh house in Cancer, malefic retrograde Jupiter is placed in the sixth house in Gemini with Venus, Mars and malefic Rahu; and malefic Ketu is placed in the twelfth house in Sagittarius with Saturn. Angarak Yoga and Guru Chandal Yoga are formed in the sixth house.

In this case, native's mother may die before his age of 10 or 5. His father may get married again, but the native may not have a good equation with his stepmother. He may not find a permanent profession till his age of 35/40, or throughout his life, though he may earn well at times. He may remain jobless for periods of more than 3 months, many times in his life. He may witness 1 or 2 failed marriages. He may lose his first wife to death. He may die before his age of 55 or 50, in an accident, due to a fatal viral infection like COVID, or he may kill himself.

Combust Moon in Eighth House in Virgo

When Sun and combust Moon are placed in the eighth house of a horoscope in Virgo, Aquarius rises in the ascendant. Sun rules the seventh house, and Moon rules the sixth house. In general, this combination is partly benefic and partly malefic here, though the malefic part is higher, in most cases. The concept of various planets exhibiting tendencies to be benefic or malefic on the basis of the houses they rule in a horoscope has been explained in the book 'Gemstones: Magic or Science?'.

Combination of Sun and combust Moon in the eighth house of horoscope in Virgo is malefic in many cases, though it may turn benefic in some cases. It may happen when such combination is influenced by one or more benefic planets, and/or an overall benefic horoscope. The concept of a malefic planet turning benefic due to influences of benefic planets has been explained in the book 'Match Making and Manglik Dosh'.

When benefic in nature, combination of Sun and combust Moon in the eighth house of a horoscope in Virgo can bless the native with good results related to father, mother, marriage, husband, wife, profession, finances, reputation, authority, recognition, fame and several other good results, depending on his/her overall horoscope and running times.

Such combination of Sun and combust Moon can render various types of benefits to the native, related to or through his

father, mother and/or marriage. Considering parents, native's father/mother may be a rich man/woman, a celebrity, an officer in government or a powerful politician. The native may enjoy many benefits because of his father/mother's money, influence and/or status. He/she may give a big amount of money, and/or wealth to the native, while he/she's alive, and/or through his/her will. Considering marriage, the native may get married to a woman who may be beautiful, rich, a celebrity, an officer in government, a powerful politician, a successful businesswoman, and/or a citizen of a foreign country. The native may witness several benefits due to or through his wife and/or her family members.

Looking at profession, such combust Moon can help the native achieve success as a fire fighter, fitness trainer, body builder, sportsman, athlete, physician, dietician, lawyer, astrologer, tantric, psychic, spiritual guru, healer, religious guru, teacher, preacher, consultant, actor, singer, musician, writer, dancer, sportsman, artist, architect, designer, developer, poet, chef, interior designer, host, researcher, analyst, professional dealing in education industry, coaching, food, health, pharma, medical, nursing, homecare, real estate, agriculture, hospitality, beauty, fashion, finance, television, music, sports, media, book, publishing, fitness, travel, hotel, airline, fishing, shipping, telecom, computer, software, IT, internet industry or some other type of professional, depending on his/her overall horoscope and running times.

Taking an example, suppose combust Moon is placed in the eighth house of a horoscope in Virgo with benefic Sun. Benefic retrograde Venus is placed in the seventh house in Leo with Mercury; benefic Jupiter is placed in the first house in Aquarius, Saturn is placed in the fourth house in Taurus, benefic debilitated Mars is placed in the sixth house in Cancer with benefic Rahu; and Ketu is placed in the twelfth house in Capricorn.

In this case, the native may become an astrologer. He may possess good knowledge of astrology, and he may come across very good amount of success, money and recognition. He may write some books on various topics of astrology, and he may also appear on some TV shows. If the finer factors and running times are supportive, he may become a very successful astrologer, and his net worth may be in multimillions.

Such combust Moon can bless the native with authority in government as a police officer, army, air force, naval, revenue, administrative, foreign services officer, judge, doctor, scientist, engineer, politician or some other type of professional. Taking an example, suppose combust Moon is placed in the eighth house of a horoscope in Virgo with benefic Sun. Benefic Venus is placed in the seventh house in Leo with Mercury and Saturn; benefic Rahu is placed in the fifth house in Gemini, Ketu is placed in the eleventh house in Sagittarius, and benefic retrograde Jupiter is placed in the sixth house in Cancer. In this case, the native may become an officer in revenue services, and he may enjoy a good career.

If benefic retrograde Mars forms Ruchaka Yoga in the tenth house in Scorpio, the equation may become better. In this case, the native may achieve success in competitive exams, and he may get selected for the highest possible direct rank in revenue services. He may serve at several important posts during his career, and he may come across very good amount of success, recognition and authority. If the finer factors and running times are supportive, he may serve as the head of a revenue department, before retirement.

On the other hand, when malefic in nature, combination of Sun and combust Moon in the eighth house of a horoscope in Virgo can trouble the native with problems related to father, mother, marriage, husband, wife, lifespan, profession, finances, reputation, authority, recognition and several other problems, depending on his/her overall horoscope and running times.

Sun rules the seventh house, Moon rules the sixth house, and they are placed in the eighth house. If such combination of Sun and combust Moon is influenced by malefic planets, and/or an overall malefic horoscope, the native may witness various types of problems related to or through his father, mother, lifespan and/or marriage. Considering parents, the native may not have a good equation with his father/mother, his parents may get divorced and he may live with his father/mother, his father/mother may suffer from a long-lasting illness, he/she may be an alcoholic and/or a drug addict, he/she may be a criminal, and/or he/she may die before native's age of 20, depending on native's overall horoscope and running times. The native may not know his biological father/mother, or his father/mother may refuse to accept him as his/her son, as native may be born from a secret love affair of his father/mother, and he/she may give him to someone else or to an orphanage. In an extreme case, the native may kill his father/mother for some reason, or his father/mother may kill him, depending on native's overall horoscope and running times. Considering marriage, the native may witness delay/disturbances in marriage, and/or one or more failed marriages. He may have serious differences of opinion with his wife, she may suffer from a long-lasting illness, she may be an alcoholic and/or a drug addict, she may be a criminal, she may not be loyal to him, she may have extramarital affair/affairs, and/or she may die within 10 or 5 years of marriage. In an extreme case, she may kill the native due to some reason, or the native may kill her, depending on native's overall horoscope and running times. Considering lifespan, the native may witness reduction in lifespan due to several reasons.

The native may witness delays, financial losses, setbacks, failures, job loss, bad reputation and several other problems related to or through his profession. Taking an example, suppose malefic combust Moon is placed in the eighth house of a horoscope in Virgo with Sun, retrograde Mercury and malefic debilitated Ketu. Malefic debilitated Rahu is placed in the second house in Pisces with retrograde Saturn; Venus is placed in the sixth house in Cancer with Jupiter; and benefic Mars is placed in the seventh house in Leo. Grahan Yoga is formed in the eighth house.

In this case, native's father may die before his age of 10 or 5. His mother may get married again, but the native may not have a good equation with his stepfather. The native may not achieve much professional success till his age of 35/40, or throughout his life. He may witness financial losses and bad reputation through profession. He may witness 1 or 2 failed marriages. He may die before his age of 50 or 45, due to drug overdose, failure of a vital organ, a heart attack, or a fatal disease.

Combust Moon in Eighth House in Libra

When Sun and combust Moon are placed in the eighth house of a horoscope in Libra, Pisces rises in the ascendant. Sun rules the sixth house, and Moon rules the fifth house. In general, this combination is partly benefic and partly malefic here, though the malefic part is higher, in most cases. The concept of various planets exhibiting tendencies to be benefic or malefic on the basis of the houses they rule in a horoscope has been explained in the book 'Gemstones: Magic or Science?'.

Combination of Sun and combust Moon in the eighth house of horoscope in Libra is malefic in many cases, though it may turn benefic in some cases. It may happen when such combination is influenced by one or more benefic planets, and/or an overall benefic horoscope. The concept of a malefic planet turning benefic due to influences of benefic planets has been explained in the book 'Match Making and Manglik Dosh'.

When benefic in nature, combination of Sun and combust Moon in the eighth house of a horoscope in Libra can bless the native with good results related to father, mother, love life, children, creativity, profession, finances, reputation, authority, recognition, fame and several other good results, depending on his/her overall horoscope and running times.

Such combination of Sun and combust Moon can render various types of benefits to the native, related to or through

his father, mother and/or children. Considering parents, native's father/mother may be a rich man/woman, a celebrity, an officer in government or a powerful politician. The native may enjoy many benefits because of his father/mother's money, influence and/or status. He/she may give a big amount of money, and/or wealth to the native, while he/she's alive, and/or through his/her will. Considering children, the native may have children who may be physically, intellectually, emotionally, creatively and/or spiritually better or much better than average.

Looking at profession, such combust Moon can help the native achieve success as a fire fighter, fitness trainer, body builder, sportsman, athlete, physician, dietician, lawyer, astrologer, tantric, psychic, spiritual guru, healer, religious guru, teacher, preacher, consultant, researcher, analyst, host, artist, poet, chef, interior designer, professional dealing in education industry, coaching, food, health, pharma, medical, nursing, homecare, real estate, agriculture, hospitality, beauty, fashion, finance, television, music, sports, media, book, publishing, fitness, travel, hotel, airline, fishing, shipping, telecom, computer, software, IT, internet industry or some other type of professional, depending on his/her overall horoscope and running times.

Such combust Moon can help the native achieve success through a creative field as an actor, singer, musician, writer, dancer, sportsman, artist, architect, designer, developer or some other likewise professional. Taking an example, suppose benefic combust Moon is placed in the eighth house of a horoscope in Libra with debilitated Sun and benefic retrograde Mercury. Benefic exalted Jupiter and benefic debilitated Mars form Neechbhang Rajyoga in the fifth house in Cancer, benefic exalted Rahu is placed in the third house in Taurus, exalted Ketu is placed in the ninth house in Scorpio, Venus is placed in the sixth house in Leo, and Saturn is placed in the seventh house in Virgo.

In this case, the native may become a music composer. He may possess remarkable talent, and he may come across very good amount of success, money, recognition and fame. He may compose music for several hit songs, and he may receive many awards. If the finer factors and running times are supportive, he may become one of the most successful music composers of his time, and his net worth may be in multimillions.

Such combust Moon can bless the native with authority in government as a police officer, army, air force, naval, revenue, administrative, foreign services officer, judge, doctor, scientist, engineer, politician or some other type of professional. Taking an example, suppose benefic combust Moon is placed in the eighth house of a horoscope in Libra with debilitated Sun and benefic Mercury. Benefic Rahu is placed in the sixth house in Leo with Venus; Ketu is placed in the twelfth house in Aquarius with Saturn; benefic Mars is placed in the seventh house in Virgo, and benefic Jupiter forms Hamsa Yoga in the tenth house in Sagittarius.

In this case, the native may achieve success in civil exams, and he may get selected for the highest possible direct rank in administrative services. He may serve at several important posts during his career, and he may come across very good amount of success, recognition and authority. If the finer factors and running times are supportive, he may serve at one of the top 2 ranks in administrative services, before retirement.

On the other hand, when malefic in nature, combination of Sun and combust Moon in the eighth house of a horoscope in Libra can trouble the native with problems related to father, mother, love life, children, lifespan, profession, finances, reputation, authority, recognition and several other problems, depending on his/her overall horoscope and running times.

Sun rules the sixth house, Moon rules the fifth house, and they are placed in the eighth house. If such combination of Sun and combust Moon is influenced by malefic planets, and/or an overall malefic horoscope, the native may witness various types of problems related to or through his father, mother, lifespan and/or children. Considering parents, the native may not have a good equation with his father/mother, his parents may get divorced and he may live with his father/mother, his father/mother may suffer from a long-lasting illness, he/she may be an alcoholic and/or a drug addict, he/she may be a criminal, and/or he/she may die before native's age of 20, depending on native's overall horoscope and running times. The native may not know his biological father/mother, or his father/mother may refuse to accept him as his/her son, as native may be born from a secret love affair of his father/mother, and he/she may give him to someone else or to an orphanage. In an extreme case, the native may kill his father/mother for some reason, or his father/mother may kill him, depending on native's overall horoscope and running times. Considering children, the native may lose one or more children through miscarriages that his wife may witness. He may witness delay in childbirth, and/or he may have children who may be physically and/or mentally troubled in some way. He may lose his children through divorce, or his children may engage in immoral/illegal activities, and he may witness bad reputation and many other problems because of them. In an extreme case, the native may witness death of one or more children during their young ages. Considering lifespan, the native may witness reduction in lifespan due to several reasons.

The native may witness delays, financial losses, setbacks, failures, job loss, bad reputation and several other problems related to or through his profession. Taking an example, suppose combust Moon is placed in the eighth house of a horoscope in Libra with Mercury, malefic Venus and malefic debilitated Sun. Malefic Rahu is placed in the tenth house in Sagittarius with malefic Saturn; malefic Ketu is placed in the fourth house in Gemini with retrograde Jupiter; and Mars is placed in the twelfth house in Aquarius. Guru Chandal Yoga is formed in the fourth house.

In this case, native's mother may die before his age of 10 or 5, and his father may die before native's age of 25 or 20. The native may not achieve much professional success till his age of 35/40, or throughout his life. He may remain jobless for periods of more than 3 months, many times in his life. He may witness 1 or 2 failed marriages. He may lose one or more children to death, through miscarriages that his wife/wives may witness. He may die before his age of 60 or 55, due to a heart attack, some type of cancer, another fatal disease, or because of a fatal viral infection like COVID.

Combust Moon in Eighth House in Scorpio

When Sun and combust Moon are placed in the eighth house of a horoscope in Scorpio, Aries rises in the ascendant. Sun rules the fifth house, and Moon rules the fourth house. In general, this combination is benefic here, in many cases. The concept of various planets exhibiting tendencies to be benefic or malefic on the basis of the houses they rule in a horoscope has been explained in the book 'Gemstones: Magic or Science?'.

Combination of Sun and combust Moon in the eighth house of horoscope in Scorpio is benefic in many cases, though it may turn malefic in some cases. It may happen when such combination is influenced by one or more malefic planets, and/or an overall malefic horoscope. The concept of a benefic planet turning malefic due to influences of malefic planets has been explained in the book 'Match Making and Manglik Dosh'.

When benefic in nature, combination of Sun and combust Moon in the eighth house of a horoscope in Scorpio can bless the native with good results related to father, mother, education, wealth, properties, vehicles, love life, children, creativity, spiritual growth, profession, finances, reputation, authority, recognition, fame and several other good results, depending on his/her overall horoscope and running times.

Such combination of Sun and combust Moon can render various types of benefits to the native, related to or through his

father, mother and/or children. Considering parents, native's father/mother may be a rich man/woman, a celebrity, an officer in government or a powerful politician. The native may enjoy many benefits because of his father/mother's money, influence and/or status. He/she may give a big amount of money, and/or wealth to the native, while he/she's alive, and/or through his/her will. This combination can bless the native with good education, vehicles, residential house/houses and/or several other good results. Considering children, the native may have children who may be physically, intellectually, emotionally, creatively and/or spiritually better or much better than average.

Looking at profession, such combust Moon can help the native achieve success as a fire fighter, fitness trainer, body builder, sportsman, athlete, physician, dietician, lawyer, astrologer, tantric, psychic, spiritual guru, healer, religious guru, teacher, preacher, consultant, researcher, analyst, host, artist, poet, chef, interior designer, professional dealing in education industry, coaching, food, health, pharma, medical, nursing, homecare, real estate, agriculture, hospitality, beauty, fashion, finance, television, music, sports, media, book, publishing, fitness, travel, hotel, airline, fishing, shipping, telecom, computer, software, IT, internet industry or some other type of professional, depending on his/her overall horoscope and running times.

Such combust Moon can help the native achieve success through a creative field as an actor, singer, musician, writer, dancer, sportsman, artist, architect, designer, developer or some other likewise professional. Taking an example, suppose benefic combust Moon is placed in the eighth house of a horoscope in Scorpio with Mercury and benefic Sun. Benefic Venus is placed in the ninth house in Sagittarius, benefic retrograde Saturn is placed in the third house in Gemini with Mars; benefic exalted Rahu is placed in the sixth house in Virgo, exalted Ketu is placed in the twelfth house in Pisces, and Jupiter is placed in the seventh house in Libra.

In this case, the native may become a professional footballer. He may possess remarkable talent related to the sport, and he may come across very good amount of success, money, recognition and fame. He may deliver several match-winning performances, and he may receive many awards/medals. If the finer factors and running times are supportive, he may become one of the most successful footballers of his time, and his net worth may be in multimillions.

Such combust Moon can bless the native with authority in government as a police officer, army, air force, naval, revenue, administrative, foreign services officer, judge, doctor, scientist, engineer, politician or some other type of professional. Taking an example, suppose benefic combust Moon is placed in the eighth house of a horoscope in Scorpio with Mercury, benefic Sun and benefic Venus. Benefic Rahu is placed in the first house in Aries, Ketu is placed in the seventh house in Libra, benefic retrograde Saturn is placed in the sixth house in Virgo, Jupiter is placed in the second house in Taurus, and exalted Mars is placed in the tenth house in Capricorn.

In this case, the native may achieve success in competitive exams, and he may get selected for the highest possible direct rank in army. He may serve at several important posts during his career, and he may come across very good amount of success, recognition and authority. If the finer factors and running times are supportive, he may serve at one of the top 2 ranks in army, before retirement.

On the other hand, when malefic in nature, combination of Sun and combust Moon in the eighth house of a horoscope in Scorpio can trouble the native with problems related to father, mother, education, wealth, properties, vehicles, love life, children, lifespan, profession, finances, reputation, authority, recognition and several other problems, depending on his/her overall horoscope and running times.

Sun rules the fifth house, Moon rules the fourth house, and they are placed in the eighth house. If such combination of Sun and combust Moon is influenced by malefic planets, and/or an overall malefic horoscope, the native may witness various types of problems related to or through his father, mother, lifespan and/or children. Considering parents, the native may not have a good equation with his father/mother, his parents may get divorced and he may live with his father/mother, his father/mother may suffer from a long-lasting illness, he/she may be an alcoholic and/or a drug addict, he/she may be a criminal, and/or he/she may die before native's age of 20, depending on native's overall horoscope and running times. The native may not know his biological father/mother, or his father/mother may refuse to accept him as his/her son, as native may be born from a secret love affair of his father/mother, and he/she may give him to someone else or to an orphanage. In an extreme case, the native may kill his father/mother for some reason, or his father/mother may kill him, depending on native's overall horoscope and running times. He may also witness various types of problems related to properties, vehicles and/or mental health. Considering children, the native may lose one or more children through miscarriages that his wife may witness. He may witness delay in childbirth, and/or he may have children who may be physically and/or mentally troubled in some way. He may lose his children through divorce, or his children may engage in immoral/illegal activities, and he may witness bad reputation and many other problems because of them. In an extreme case, the native may witness death of one or more children during their young ages. Considering lifespan, the native may witness reduction in lifespan due to several reasons.

The native may witness delays, financial losses, setbacks, failures, job loss, bad reputation and several other problems related to or through his profession. Taking an example, suppose combust Moon is placed in the eighth house of a horoscope in Scorpio with Sun, Mars and malefic retrograde Mercury. Malefic Rahu is placed in the third house in Gemini with Jupiter; malefic Ketu is placed in the ninth house in Sagittarius, and debilitated Venus is placed in the sixth house in Virgo with Saturn. Guru Chandal Yoga is formed in the third house.

In this case, native's mother may die before his age of 10 or 5, and his father may die before native's age of 20 or 15. The native may not achieve much professional success till his age of 35/40, or throughout his life, though he may earn well at times. He may witness failures and financial losses through profession. He may not get married till his age of 35/40, or throughout his life. He may not have a child till his age of 40/45, or throughout his life. He may die before his age of 60 or 55, due to a heart attack, in an accident, because of a fatal viral infection like COVID, or someone may kill him.

Combust Moon in Eighth House in Sagittarius

When Sun and combust Moon are placed in the eighth house of a horoscope in Sagittarius, Taurus rises in the ascendant. Sun rules the fourth house, and Moon rules the third house. In general, this combination is benefic here, in many cases. The concept of various planets exhibiting tendencies to be benefic or malefic on the basis of the houses they rule in a horoscope has been explained in the book 'Gemstones: Magic or Science?'.

Combination of Sun and combust Moon in the eighth house of horoscope in Sagittarius is benefic in many cases, though it may turn malefic in some cases. It may happen when such combination is influenced by one or more malefic planets, and/or an overall malefic horoscope. The concept of a benefic planet turning malefic due to influences of malefic planets has been explained in the book 'Match Making and Manglik Dosh'.

When benefic in nature, combination of Sun and combust Moon in the eighth house of a horoscope in Sagittarius can bless the native with good results related to father, mother, education, wealth, properties, vehicles, siblings, colleagues, profession, finances, reputation, authority, recognition, fame and several other good results, depending on his/her overall horoscope and running times.

Such combination of Sun and combust Moon can render various types of benefits to the native, related to or through his father, mother and/or siblings. Considering parents, native's father/mother may be a rich man/woman, a celebrity, an officer in government or a powerful politician. The native may enjoy many benefits because of his father/mother's money, influence and/or status. He/she may give a big amount of money, and/or wealth to the native, while he/she's alive, and/or through his/her will. This combination can bless the native with good education, vehicles, residential house/houses and/or several other good results. Considering siblings, some of them may stand by the native and they may help him get out of his problems, many times in his life. A sibling of the native may give him a big amount of money, and/or wealth, while such sibling is alive, and/or through his/her will.

Looking at profession, such combust Moon can help the native achieve success as a fire fighter, fitness trainer, body builder, sportsman, athlete, physician, dietician, lawyer, astrologer, tantric, psychic, spiritual guru, healer, religious guru, teacher, preacher, consultant, researcher, analyst, host, artist, poet, chef, interior designer, professional dealing in education industry, coaching, food, health, pharma, medical, nursing, homecare, real estate, agriculture, hospitality, beauty, fashion, finance, television, music, sports, media, book, publishing, fitness, travel, hotel, airline, fishing, shipping, telecom, computer, software, IT, internet industry or some other type of professional, depending on his/her overall horoscope and running times.

Such combust Moon can help the native achieve success as an actor, singer, musician, writer, dancer, sportsman, artist, architect, designer, developer or some other likewise professional. Taking an example, suppose benefic combust Moon is placed in the eighth house of a horoscope in

Sagittarius with benefic Sun and benefic Mercury. Benefic Rahu is placed in the ninth house in Capricorn with Venus; Ketu is placed in the third house in Cancer, benefic Saturn forms Shasha Yoga in the tenth house in Aquarius, Mars is placed in the fifth house in Virgo, and Jupiter is placed in the sixth house in Libra. Sun and Mercury form Budhaditya Yoga in the eighth house.

In this case, the native may become a professional boxer. He may possess remarkable talent related to the sport, and he may come across very good amount of success, money, recognition and fame. He may win majority of his matches, as well as several championship titles. If the finer factors and running times are supportive, he may become world heavyweight boxing champion, and his net worth may be in multimillions.

Such combust Moon can bless the native with authority in government as a police officer, army, air force, naval, revenue, administrative, foreign services officer, judge, doctor, scientist, engineer, politician or some other type of professional. Taking an example, suppose benefic combust Moon is placed in the eighth house of a horoscope in Sagittarius with benefic Sun. Benefic Mercury is placed in the ninth house in Capricorn with Venus; retrograde Jupiter is placed in the tenth house in Aquarius, benefic Rahu is placed in the sixth house in Libra with Mars; and Ketu is placed in the twelfth house in Aries. In this case, the native may engage in politics, and he may become a minister in a state government.

If benefic Saturn is placed in the ninth house in Capricorn with Mercury and Venus; the equation may become better. In this case, the native may come across very good amount of success, recognition, authority and fame through politics. He may win several elections, and he may become chief minister or governor of a state. If the finer factors and running times are supportive, he may hold one such post, more than once in his life.

On the other hand, when malefic in nature, combination of Sun and combust Moon in the eighth house of a horoscope in Sagittarius can trouble the native with problems related to father, mother, education, wealth, properties, vehicles, siblings, colleagues, lifespan, profession, finances, reputation, authority, recognition and several other problems, depending on his/her overall horoscope and running times.

Sun rules the fourth house, Moon rules the third house, and they are placed in the eighth house. If such combination of Sun and combust Moon is influenced by malefic planets, and/or an overall malefic horoscope, the native may witness various types of problems related to or through his father, mother, lifespan and/or siblings. Considering parents, the native may not have a good equation with his father/mother, his parents may get divorced and he may live with his father/mother, his father/mother may suffer from a long-lasting illness, he/she may be an alcoholic and/or a drug addict, he/she may be a criminal, and/or he/she may die before native's age of 20, depending on native's overall horoscope and running times. The native may not know his biological father/mother, or his father/mother may refuse to accept him as his/her son, as native may be born from a secret love affair of his father/mother, and he/she may give him to someone else or to an orphanage. In an extreme case, the native may kill his father/mother for some reason, or his father/mother may kill him, depending on native's overall horoscope and running times. He may also witness various types of problems related to properties, vehicles and/or mental health. Considering siblings, the native may face several problems because of some of them. In an extreme case, the native may lose one or more siblings to death, before his age of 40 or 35. Considering lifespan, the native may witness reduction in lifespan due to several reasons.

The native may witness delays, financial losses, setbacks, failures, job loss, bad reputation and several other problems related to or through his profession. Taking an example, suppose combust Moon is placed in the eighth house of a horoscope in Sagittarius with Sun, malefic Jupiter and malefic Mars. Malefic Rahu is placed in the twelfth house in Aries with debilitated Saturn; malefic Ketu is placed in the sixth house in Libra with Venus; and benefic Mercury is placed in the seventh house in Scorpio.

In this case, native's father as well as mother may die before his age of 15 or 10. The native may not find a permanent profession throughout his life, and he may only find temporary jobs. He may remain jobless for periods of more than 3 months, many times in his life. He may lose one or more siblings to death, before his age of 35 or 30. He may not get married till his age of 35/40, or throughout his life. He may die before his age of 55 or 50, due to a heart attack, in an accident, because of a fatal viral infection like COVID, or someone may kill him.

Combust Moon in Eighth House in Capricorn

When Sun and combust Moon are placed in the eighth house of a horoscope in Capricorn, Gemini rises in the ascendant. Sun rules the third house, and Moon rules the second house. In general, this combination is benefic here, in many cases. The concept of various planets exhibiting tendencies to be benefic or malefic on the basis of the houses they rule in a horoscope has been explained in the book 'Gemstones: Magic or Science?'.

Combination of Sun and combust Moon in the eighth house of horoscope in Capricorn is benefic in many cases, though it may turn malefic in some cases. It may happen when such combination is influenced by one or more malefic planets, and/or an overall malefic horoscope. The concept of a benefic planet turning malefic due to influences of malefic planets has been explained in the book 'Match Making and Manglik Dosh'.

When benefic in nature, combination of Sun and combust Moon in the eighth house of a horoscope in Capricorn can bless the native with good results related to father, mother, family, wealth, speech, siblings, colleagues, profession, finances, reputation, authority, recognition, fame and several other good results, depending on his/her overall horoscope and running times.

Such combination of Sun and combust Moon can render various types of benefits to the native, related to or through his father, mother, siblings and/or family. Considering parents, native's father/mother may be a rich man/woman, a celebrity, an officer in government or a powerful politician. The native may enjoy many benefits because of his father/mother's money, influence and/or status. He/she may give a big amount of money, and/or wealth to the native, while he/she's alive, and/or through his/her will. Considering siblings, some of them may stand by the native and they may help him get out of his problems, many times in his life. A sibling of the native may give him a big amount of money, and/or wealth, while such sibling is alive, and/or through his/her will.

Looking at profession, such combust Moon can help the native achieve success as a fire fighter, fitness trainer, body builder, sportsman, athlete, physician, dietician, lawyer, astrologer, tantric, psychic, spiritual guru, healer, religious guru, teacher, preacher, consultant, researcher, analyst, host, artist, poet, chef, interior designer, professional dealing in education industry, coaching, food, health, pharma, medical, nursing, homecare, real estate, agriculture, hospitality, beauty, fashion, finance, television, music, sports, media, book, publishing, fitness, travel, hotel, airline, fishing, shipping, telecom, computer, software, IT, internet industry or some other type of professional, depending on his/her overall horoscope and running times.

Such combust Moon can help the native achieve success as an actor, singer, musician, writer, dancer, sportsman, artist, architect, designer, developer or some other likewise professional. Taking an example for a female native, suppose benefic combust Moon is placed in the eighth house of a horoscope in Capricorn with Venus and benefic Sun. Benefic Mercury is placed in the seventh house in Sagittarius, benefic retrograde Jupiter is placed in the fourth house in Virgo, Mars is placed in the eleventh house in Aries, benefic debilitated Rahu is placed in the sixth house in Scorpio with Saturn; and debilitated Ketu is placed in the twelfth house in Taurus.

In this case, the native may become a professional swimmer. She may possess remarkable talent related to the sport, and she may come across very good amount of success, money, recognition and fame. She may win several medals/ awards, and championship titles. If the finer factors and running times are supportive, she may become one of the most successful swimmers of her time, and her net worth may be in multimillions.

Such combust Moon can bless the native with authority in government as a police officer, army, air force, naval, revenue, administrative, foreign services officer, judge, doctor, scientist, engineer, politician or some other type of professional. Taking an example, suppose benefic combust Moon is placed in the eighth house of a horoscope in Capricorn with Venus and benefic Sun. Benefic debilitated Rahu is placed in the sixth house in Scorpio with Mars; debilitated Ketu is placed in the twelfth house in Taurus, retrograde Saturn is placed in the first house in Gemini, and benefic retrograde Mercury is placed in the ninth house in Aquarius. In this case, the native may become an officer in police force, and he may enjoy a good career.

If benefic Jupiter forms Hamsa Yoga in the seventh house in Sagittarius, the equation may become better. In this case, the native may achieve success in civil exams, and he may get selected for the highest possible direct rank in police force. He may serve at several important posts during his career, and he may come across very good amount of success, recognition and authority. If the finer factors and running times are supportive, he may serve as the chief of police of a state, before retirement.

On the other hand, when malefic in nature, combination of Sun and combust Moon in the eighth house of a horoscope in Capricorn can trouble the native with problems related to father, mother, family, wealth, speech, siblings, colleagues, lifespan, profession, finances, reputation, authority, recognition and several other problems, depending on his/her overall horoscope and running times.

Sun rules the third house, Moon rules the second house, and they are placed in the eighth house. If such combination of Sun and combust Moon is influenced by malefic planets, and/or an overall malefic horoscope, the native may witness various types of problems related to or through his father, mother, lifespan, siblings and/or family. Considering parents, the native may not have a good equation with his father/mother, his parents may get divorced and he may live with his father/mother, his father/mother may suffer from a long-lasting illness, he/she may be an alcoholic and/or a drug addict, he/she may be a criminal, and/or he/she may die before native's age of 20, depending on native's overall horoscope and running times. The native may not know his biological father/mother, or his father/mother may refuse to accept him as his/her son, as native may be born from a secret love affair of his father/mother, and he/she may give him to someone else or to an orphanage. In an extreme case, the native may kill his father/mother for some reason, or his father/mother may kill him, depending on native's overall horoscope and running times. Considering siblings, the native may have bad relationships with some of his siblings, and/or he may witness various types of problems through them or due to them. In an extreme case, the native may lose one or more siblings to death, before his age of 40 or 35. Considering lifespan, the native may witness reduction in lifespan due to several reasons.

The native may witness delays, financial losses, setbacks, failures, job loss, bad reputation and several other problems related to or through his profession. Taking an example, suppose combust Moon is placed in the eighth house of a horoscope in Capricorn with Sun, malefic Rahu and malefic exalted Mars. Malefic Ketu is placed in the second house in Cancer with retrograde Saturn; Venus is placed in the seventh house in Sagittarius with retrograde Mercury; and Jupiter is placed in the sixth house in Scorpio. Grahan Yoga is formed in the eighth house.

In this case, native's father may die before native's age of 10 or 5, and his mother may die before his age of 20 or 15. He may not find a permanent profession till his age of 35/40, or throughout his life, though he may earn well at times. He may witness financial losses and bad reputation through profession. He may lose one or more siblings to death, before his age of 35 or 30. He may witness 1 or 2 failed marriages. He may die before his age of 60 or 55, due to a heart attack, some type of cancer, in an accident, or someone may kill him.

Combust Moon in Eighth House in Aquarius

When Sun and combust Moon are placed in the eighth house of a horoscope in Aquarius, Cancer rises in the ascendant. Sun rules the second house, and Moon rules the first house. In general, this combination is benefic here, in many cases. The concept of various planets exhibiting tendencies to be benefic or malefic on the basis of the houses they rule in a horoscope has been explained in the book 'Gemstones: Magic or Science?'.

Combination of Sun and combust Moon in the eighth house of horoscope in Aquarius is benefic in many cases, though it may turn malefic in some cases. It may happen when such combination is influenced by one or more malefic planets, and/or an overall malefic horoscope. The concept of a benefic planet turning malefic due to influences of malefic planets has been explained in the book 'Match Making and Manglik Dosh'.

When benefic in nature, combination of Sun and combust Moon in the eighth house of a horoscope in Aquarius can bless the native with good results related to father, mother, health, lifespan, family, wealth, speech, profession, finances, reputation, authority, recognition, fame and several other good results, depending on his/her overall horoscope and running times.

Such combination of Sun and combust Moon can render various types of benefits to the native, related to or through his father, mother, family and/or lifespan. Considering parents, native's father/mother may be a rich man/woman, a celebrity, an officer in government or a powerful politician. The native may enjoy many benefits because of his father/mother's money, influence and/or status. He/she may give a big amount of money, and/or wealth to the native, while he/she's alive, and/or through his/her will. Considering family, the native may be born in a rich, influential, resourceful, well-respected, politically powerful, royal and/or spiritually advanced family, and he may witness several benefits by virtue of being a member of such family. The native may be a good, very good or gifted speaker, and he may achieve good results in many spheres of his life, by virtue of his speech abilities.

Looking at profession, such combust Moon can help the native achieve success as a fire fighter, fitness trainer, body builder, sportsman, athlete, physician, dietician, lawyer, astrologer, tantric, psychic, spiritual guru, healer, religious guru, teacher, preacher, consultant, researcher, analyst, host, artist, poet, chef, interior designer, police officer, army, air force, naval, revenue, administrative, foreign services officer, judge, doctor, scientist, engineer, politician, professional dealing in education industry, coaching, food, health, pharma, medical, nursing, homecare, real estate, agriculture, hospitality, beauty, fashion, finance, television, music, sports, media, book, publishing, fitness, travel, hotel, airline, fishing, shipping, telecom, computer, software, IT, internet industry or some other type of professional, depending on his/her overall horoscope and running times.

Taking an example, suppose benefic combust Moon is placed in the eighth house of a horoscope in Aquarius with Saturn and benefic Sun. Mercury is placed in the seventh house in Capricorn, benefic Mars is placed in the sixth house in Sagittarius with benefic Venus; benefic exalted Rahu is placed in the eleventh house in Taurus, exalted Ketu is placed in the fifth house in Scorpio, and Jupiter is placed in the second house in Leo.

In this case, the native may start a company which may make various types of packed food products, and he may come across very good amount of success, money and recognition. His business may expand after his age of 35/40, and it may keep growing. If the finer factors and running times are supportive, he may own a business empire worth in billions, by his age of 55/60.

Such combust Moon can help the native achieve success through a creative field as an actor, singer, musician, writer, dancer, sportsman, artist, architect, designer, developer or some other likewise professional. Taking an example, suppose benefic combust Moon is placed in the eighth house of a horoscope in Aquarius with benefic Sun. Benefic exalted Rahu is placed in the eleventh house in Taurus, exalted Ketu is placed in the fifth house in Scorpio, benefic exalted Venus is placed in the ninth house in Pisces with Jupiter; Mercury is placed in the seventh house in Capricorn, and Saturn is placed in the fourth house in Libra. In this case, the native may become a singer, and he may witness good results.

If benefic Mars is placed in the eleventh house in Taurus with Rahu, the equation may become better. The native may possess remarkable singing talent, and he may come across very good amount of success, money, recognition and fame. He may deliver several hit songs, and he may receive many awards. If the finer factors and running times are supportive, he may become one of the most successful singers of his time, and his net worth may be in multimillions.

On the other hand, when malefic in nature, combination of Sun and combust Moon in the eighth house of a horoscope in Aquarius can trouble the native with problems related to father, mother, family, wealth, speech, health, lifespan, profession, finances, reputation, authority, recognition and several other problems, depending on his/her overall horoscope and running times.

Sun rules the second house, Moon rules the first house, and they are placed in the eighth house. If such combination of Sun and combust Moon is influenced by malefic planets, and/or an overall malefic horoscope, the native may witness various types of problems related to or through his father, mother, lifespan and/or family. Considering parents, the native may not have a good equation with his father/mother, his parents may get divorced and he may live with his father/mother, his father/mother may suffer from a long-lasting illness, he/she may be an alcoholic and/or a drug addict, he/she may be a criminal, and/or he/she may die before native's age of 20, depending on native's overall horoscope and running times. The native may not know his biological father/mother, or his father/mother may refuse to accept him as his/her son, as native may be born from a secret love affair of his father/mother, and he/she may give him to someone else or to an orphanage. In an extreme case, the native may kill his father/mother for some reason, or his father/mother may kill him, depending on native's overall horoscope and running times. Considering lifespan, the native may witness reduction in lifespan due to several reasons. For example, the native may die in an accident, through a natural disaster, due to a fatal disease, due to a fatal viral infection like COVID, due to drug addiction, he may commit suicide, or someone may kill him intentionally or unintentionally.

The native may witness delays, financial losses, setbacks, failures, job loss, bad reputation and several other problems related to or through his profession. Taking an example, suppose combust Moon is placed in the eighth house of a horoscope in Aquarius with Sun, malefic Mercury and malefic retrograde Saturn. Malefic debilitated Rahu is placed in the ninth house in Pisces with exalted Venus; malefic debilitated Ketu is placed in the third house in Virgo, Jupiter is placed in the twelfth house in Taurus, and Mars is placed in the sixth house in Sagittarius.

In this case, native's father may die before native's age of 10 or 5. His mother may get married again, but the native may not have a good equation with his stepfather. He may not achieve much professional success throughout his life, though he may earn well at times. He may remain jobless for periods of more than 3 months, many times in his life. He may witness 1 or 2 failed marriages. He may die before his age of 50 or 45, due to drug overdose, a heart attack, failure of a vital body organ, or because of a fatal viral infection like COVID.

Combust Moon in Eighth House in Pisces

When Sun and combust Moon are placed in the eighth house of a horoscope in Pisces, Leo rises in the ascendant. Sun rules the first house, and Moon rules the twelfth house. In general, this combination is partly benefic and partly malefic here, though the malefic part is higher, in most cases. The concept of various planets exhibiting tendencies to be benefic or malefic on the basis of the houses they rule in a horoscope has been explained in the book 'Gemstones: Magic or Science?'.

Combination of Sun and combust Moon in the eighth house of horoscope in Pisces is malefic in many cases, though it may turn benefic in some cases. It may happen when such combination is influenced by one or more benefic planets, and/or an overall benefic horoscope. The concept of a malefic planet turning benefic due to influences of benefic planets has been explained in the book 'Match Making and Manglik Dosh'.

When benefic in nature, combination of Sun and combust Moon in the eighth house of a horoscope in Pisces can bless the native with good results related to father, mother, health, lifespan, creativity, spiritual growth, profession, finances, reputation, authority, recognition, fame and several other good results, depending on his/her overall horoscope and running times.

Such combination of Sun and combust Moon can render various types of benefits to the native, related to or through his

father, mother and/or lifespan. Considering parents, native's father/mother may be a rich man/woman, a celebrity, an officer in government or a powerful politician. The native may enjoy many benefits because of his father/mother's money, influence and/or status. He/she may give a big amount of money, and/or wealth to the native, while he/she's alive, and/or through his/her will.

Looking at profession, such combust Moon can help the native achieve success as a fire fighter, fitness trainer, body builder, sportsman, athlete, physician, dietician, lawyer, astrologer, tantric, psychic, spiritual guru, healer, religious guru, teacher, preacher, consultant, actor, singer, musician, writer, dancer, sportsman, artist, architect, designer, developer, poet, chef, interior designer, host, researcher, analyst, professional dealing in education industry, coaching, food, health, pharma, medical, nursing, homecare, real estate, agriculture, hospitality, beauty, fashion, finance, television, music, sports, media, book, publishing, fitness, travel, hotel, airline, fishing, shipping, telecom, computer, software, IT, internet industry or some other type of professional, depending on his/her overall horoscope and running times.

Taking an example, suppose combust Moon is placed in the eighth house of a horoscope in Pisces with benefic Sun. Benefic Venus is placed in the tenth house in Taurus with benefic retrograde Mars; benefic Rahu is placed in the eleventh house in Gemini, Ketu is placed in the fifth house in Sagittarius, retrograde Jupiter is placed in the twelfth house in Cancer, and Saturn is placed in the seventh house in Aquarius. Venus forms Malavya Yoga in the tenth house. In this case, the native may start an airline, and he may witness good results.

If benefic Mercury is placed in the ninth house in Aries, the equation may become better. In this case, the native may come across very good amount of success, money and recognition through aviation industry. His business may expand after his age of 40/45, and it may keep growing. If the finer factors and running times are supportive, he may own a business empire worth in billions, by his age of 55/60.

Such combust Moon can bless the native with authority in government as a police officer, army, air force, naval, revenue, administrative, foreign services officer, judge, doctor, scientist, engineer, politician or some other type of professional. Taking an example, suppose combust Moon is placed in the eighth house of a horoscope in Pisces with benefic Sun and benefic exalted Venus. Benefic retrograde Mercury is placed in the ninth house in Aries, benefic Rahu is placed in the first house in Leo, Ketu is placed in the seventh house in Aquarius, Saturn is placed in the sixth house in Capricorn, and Jupiter is placed in the fourth house in Scorpio. In this case, the native may become an officer in foreign services of his country, and he may enjoy a good career.

If benefic Mars is placed in the tenth house in Taurus, the equation may become better. In this case, the native may achieve success in civil exams, and he may get selected for the highest possible direct rank in foreign services. He may serve at several important posts during his career, and he may come across very good amount of success, recognition and authority. He may represent his country in several countries of the world. If the finer factors and running times are supportive, he may serve at one of the top 2 ranks in foreign services, before retirement.

On the other hand, when malefic in nature, combination of Sun and combust Moon in the eighth house of a horoscope in Pisces can trouble the native with problems related to father, mother, health, lifespan, profession, finances, reputation, authority, recognition and several other problems, depending on his/her overall horoscope and running times.

Sun rules the first house, Moon rules the twelfth house, and they are placed in the eighth house. If such combination of Sun and combust Moon is influenced by malefic planets, and/or an overall malefic horoscope, the native may witness various types of problems related to or through his father, mother and/or lifespan. Considering parents, the native may not have a good equation with his father/mother, his parents may get divorced and he may live with his father/mother, his father/mother may suffer from a long-lasting illness, he/she may be an alcoholic and/or a drug addict, he/she may be a criminal, and/or he/she may die before native's age of 20, depending on native's overall horoscope and running times. The native may not know his biological father/mother, or his father/mother may refuse to accept him as his/her son, as native may be born from a secret love affair of his father/ mother, and he/she may give him to someone else or to an orphanage. In an extreme case, the native may kill his father/ mother for some reason, or his father/mother may kill him, depending on native's overall horoscope and running times. Considering lifespan, the native may witness reduction in lifespan due to several reasons. For example, the native may die in an accident, through a natural disaster, due to a fatal disease, due to a fatal viral infection like COVID, due to drug addiction, he may commit suicide, or someone may kill him intentionally or unintentionally.

The native may witness delays, financial losses, setbacks, failures, job loss, bad reputation and several other problems related to or through his profession. Taking an example, suppose malefic combust Moon is placed in the eighth house of a horoscope in Pisces with Sun, exalted Venus and malefic exalted Ketu. Malefic exalted Rahu is placed in the second house in Virgo, retrograde Jupiter is placed in the twelfth house in Cancer with debilitated Mars; and malefic Saturn is placed in the seventh house in Aquarius with Mercury. Grahan Yoga is formed in the eighth house.

In this case, native's father as well as mother may die before his age of 15 or 10. He may witness a troublesome childhood. He may not find a permanent profession throughout his life, and he may only find temporary jobs. He may remain jobless for periods of more than 6 months, many times in his life. He may not get married till his age of 35/40, or throughout his life. He may die before his age of 60 or 55, due to a heart attack, some type of cancer, another fatal disease, or because of a fatal viral infection like COVID.

Combust Moon in Ninth House in Aries

When Sun and combust Moon are placed in the ninth house of a horoscope in Aries, Leo rises in the ascendant. Sun rules the first house, and Moon rules the twelfth house. In general, this combination is partly benefic and partly malefic here, though the benefic part is higher, in most cases. The concept of various planets exhibiting tendencies to be benefic or malefic on the basis of the houses they rule in a horoscope has been explained in the book 'Gemstones: Magic or Science?'.

Combination of Sun and combust Moon in the ninth house of horoscope in Aries is benefic in many cases, though it may turn malefic in some cases. It may happen when such combination is influenced by one or more malefic planets, and/or an overall malefic horoscope. The concept of a benefic planet turning malefic due to influences of malefic planets has been explained in the book 'Match Making and Manglik Dosh'.

When benefic in nature, combination of Sun and combust Moon in the ninth house of a horoscope in Aries can bless the native with good results related to father, mother, creativity, spiritual growth, health, lifespan, profession, finances, reputation, authority, recognition, fame and several other good results, depending on his/her overall horoscope and running times.

Such combination of Sun and combust Moon can render various types of benefits to the native, related to or through his father, mother and/or lifespan. Considering parents, native's father/mother may be a rich man/woman, a celebrity, an officer in government or a powerful politician. The native may enjoy many benefits because of his father/ mother's money, influence and/or status. He/she may give a big amount of money, and/or wealth to the native, while he/ she's alive, and/or through his/her will. Such combination of Sun and combust Moon can render creativity, bravery, courage, leadership abilities and business skills to the native, among other things. Hence, he may achieve success through a wide variety of jobs, and/or businesses. It can also bless the native with good health and a long life, like beyond 70, 80 or 90, depending on his overall horoscope and running times.

Looking at profession, such combust Moon can help the native achieve success as a fire fighter, fitness trainer, body builder, sportsman, athlete, physician, dietician, lawyer, astrologer, tantric, psychic, spiritual guru, healer, religious guru, teacher, preacher, consultant, researcher, analyst, host, artist, poet, chef, interior designer, professional dealing in education industry, coaching, food, health, pharma, medical, nursing, homecare, real estate, agriculture, hospitality, beauty, fashion, finance, television, music, sports, media, book, publishing, fitness, travel, hotel, airline, fishing, shipping, telecom, computer, software, IT, internet industry or some other type of professional, depending on his/her overall horoscope and running times.

Such combust Moon can help the native achieve success through a creative field as an actor, singer, musician, writer, dancer, sportsman, artist, architect, designer, developer or some other likewise professional. Taking an example, suppose combust Moon is placed in the ninth house of a horoscope in Aries with benefic exalted Sun and benefic retrograde Mercury. Benefic Venus is placed in the tenth house in Taurus, benefic Rahu is placed in the eleventh house in Gemini, Ketu is placed in the fifth house in Sagittarius, Jupiter is placed in the fourth house in Scorpio, and Saturn is placed in the eighth house in Pisces. In this case, the native may become a singer, and he may witness good results.

If benefic Mars is placed in the second house in Virgo, the equation may become better. The native may possess remarkable singing talent, and he may come across very good amount of success, money, recognition and fame. He may deliver several hit songs, and he may receive many awards. If the finer factors and running times are supportive, he may become one of the most successful singers of his time, and his net worth may be in multimillions.

Such combust Moon can bless the native with authority in government as a police officer, army, air force, naval, revenue, administrative, foreign services officer, judge, doctor, scientist, engineer, politician or some other type of professional. Taking an example, suppose combust Moon is placed in the ninth house of a horoscope in Aries with benefic Venus, benefic Mercury and benefic exalted Sun. Benefic retrograde Mars is placed in the eighth house in Pisces with Jupiter; benefic Rahu is placed in the fifth house in Sagittarius, and Ketu is placed in the eleventh house in Gemini with Saturn.

In this case, the native may achieve success in civil exams, and he may get selected for the highest possible direct rank in revenue services. He may serve at several important posts during his career, and he may come across very good amount of success, recognition and authority. If the finer factors and running times are supportive, he may serve as the head of a revenue department, before retirement.

On the other hand, when malefic in nature, combination of Sun and combust Moon in the ninth house of a horoscope in Aries can trouble the native with problems related to father, mother, health, lifespan, profession, finances, reputation, authority, recognition and several other problems, depending on his/her overall horoscope and running times.

Sun rules the first house, Moon rules the twelfth house, and they are placed in the ninth house. If such combination of Sun and combust Moon is influenced by malefic planets, and/or an overall malefic horoscope, the native may witness various types of problems related to or through his father, mother and/or lifespan. Considering parents, the native may not have a good equation with his father/mother, his parents may get divorced and he may live with his father/mother, his father/mother may suffer from a long-lasting illness, he/she may be an alcoholic and/or a drug addict, he/she may be a criminal, and/or he/she may die before native's age of 20, depending on native's overall horoscope and running times. Considering lifespan, the native may witness reduction in lifespan due to several reasons. For example, the native may die in an accident, through a natural disaster, due to a fatal disease, due to a fatal viral infection like COVID, due to drug addiction, he may commit suicide, or someone may kill him intentionally or unintentionally. Considering some unintentional incidents, he may get caught in a crossfire between two rival criminal gangs or that between criminals and police, or someone may accidently kill him.

The native may witness delays, financial losses, setbacks, failures, job loss, bad reputation and several other problems related to or through his profession. Taking an example, suppose malefic combust Moon is placed in the ninth house of a horoscope in Aries with exalted Sun, Jupiter and malefic Rahu. Malefic Ketu is placed in the third house in Libra with Mars; debilitated Mercury is placed in the eighth house in Pisces, benefic Venus is placed in the seventh house in Aquarius, and malefic retrograde Saturn is placed in the sixth house in Capricorn. Grahan Yoga and Guru Chandal Yoga are formed in the ninth house.

In this case, native's father may die before native's age of 10 or 5. His mother may get married again, but the native may not have a good equation with his stepfather. The native may not achieve much professional success till his age of 35/40, or throughout his life. He may witness financial tightness and debts, many times in his life. He may remain jobless for periods of more than 3 months, many times in his life. He may witness 1 or 2 failed marriages. He may die before his age of 60 or 55, due to a heart attack, in an accident, or because of a fatal viral infection like COVID.

Combust Moon in Ninth House in Taurus

When Sun and combust Moon are placed in the ninth house of a horoscope in Taurus, Virgo rises in the ascendant. Sun rules the twelfth house, and Moon rules the eleventh house. In general, this combination is partly benefic and partly malefic here, though the benefic part is higher, in most cases. The concept of various planets exhibiting tendencies to be benefic or malefic on the basis of the houses they rule in a horoscope has been explained in the book 'Gemstones: Magic or Science?'.

Combination of Sun and combust Moon in the ninth house of horoscope in Taurus is benefic in many cases, though it may turn malefic in some cases. It may happen when such combination is influenced by one or more malefic planets, and/or an overall malefic horoscope. The concept of a benefic planet turning malefic due to influences of malefic planets has been explained in the book 'Match Making and Manglik Dosh'.

When benefic in nature, combination of Sun and combust Moon in the ninth house of a horoscope in Taurus can bless the native with good results related to father, mother, creativity, spiritual growth, friends, profession, finances, reputation, authority, recognition, fame and several other good results, depending on his/her overall horoscope and running times.

Such combination of Sun and combust Moon can render various types of benefits to the native, related to or through his father, mother and/or friends. Considering parents, native's

father/mother may be a rich man/woman, a celebrity, an officer in government or a powerful politician. The native may enjoy many benefits because of his father/mother's money, influence and/or status. He/she may give a big amount of money, and/or wealth to the native, while he/she's alive, and/ or through his/her will. Considering friends, some of his friends may stand by the native and they may help him get out of his problems, many times in his life. One or more of his friends may help him financially as well as in other ways, in order for him to start a new business, or repair/consolidate an already existing business.

Looking at profession, such combust Moon can help the native achieve success as a fire fighter, fitness trainer, body builder, sportsman, athlete, physician, dietician, lawyer, astrologer, tantric, psychic, spiritual guru, healer, religious guru, teacher, preacher, consultant, researcher, analyst, host, artist, poet, chef, interior designer, police officer, army, air force, naval, revenue, administrative, foreign services officer, judge, doctor, scientist, engineer, politician, professional dealing in education industry, coaching, food, health, pharma, medical, nursing, homecare, real estate, agriculture, hospitality, beauty, fashion, finance, television, music, sports, media, book, publishing, fitness, travel, hotel, airline, fishing, shipping, telecom, computer, software, IT, internet industry or some other type of professional, depending on his/her overall horoscope and running times.

Taking an example, suppose benefic combust Moon is placed in the ninth house of a horoscope in Taurus with Sun, Saturn and benefic retrograde Mercury. Benefic Venus is placed in the eighth house in Aries, debilitated Mars is placed in the eleventh house in Cancer, benefic Rahu is placed in the twelfth house in Leo, and Ketu is placed in the sixth house in Aquarius. In this case, the native may get a well-paying job in a well-established bank, and he may witness good results.

If benefic Jupiter is placed in the tenth house in Gemini, the equation may become better. In this case, the native may come across very good amount of success, money and recognition through banking industry. He may accomplish a lot during his career, and he may keep getting promoted on regular basis. If the finer factors and running times are supportive, he may serve as CEO or Chairman of such bank, for several years. His net worth may be in multimillions.

Such combust Moon can help the native achieve success through a creative field as an actor, singer, musician, writer, dancer, sportsman, artist, architect, designer, developer or some other likewise professional. Taking an example for a female native, suppose benefic combust Moon is placed in the ninth house of a horoscope in Taurus with Sun and benefic Mercury. Benefic Venus is placed in the tenth house in Gemini, benefic Rahu is placed in the second house in Libra, Ketu is placed in the eighth house in Aries, Mars is placed in the seventh house in Pisces, and retrograde Saturn is placed in the third house in Scorpio. In this case, the native may become an actor, and she may witness good results.

If benefic retrograde Jupiter is placed in the ninth house in Taurus with Sun, Moon and Mercury; the equation may become better. Jupiter and Moon form Gaj Kesari Yoga in the ninth house. The native may possess remarkable acting talent, and she may come across very good amount of success, money, recognition and fame. She may perform very well in the genres of romance, drama and comedy. She may deliver several hit movies, and she may receive many awards. If the finer factors and running times are supportive, she may become one of the most successful actors of her time, and her net worth may be in multimillions.

On the other hand, when malefic in nature, combination of Sun and combust Moon in the ninth house of a horoscope in Taurus can trouble the native with problems related to father, mother, friends, profession, finances, reputation, authority, recognition and several other problems, depending on his/her overall horoscope and running times.

Sun rules the twelfth house, Moon rules the eleventh house, and they are placed in the ninth house. If such combination of Sun and combust Moon is influenced by malefic planets, and/or an overall malefic horoscope, the native may witness various types of problems related to or through his father, mother and/or friends. Considering parents, the native may not have a good equation with his father/mother, his parents may get divorced and he may live with his father/mother, his father/mother may suffer from a long-lasting illness, he/she may be an alcoholic and/or a drug addict, he/she may be a criminal, and/or he/she may die before native's age of 20, depending on native's overall horoscope and running times. Considering friends, some of his friends may be selfish, opportunists, criminal-minded, criminals, drug addicts, traitors and/or they may have some other negative traits. The native may witness several problems because of such friends, many times in his life. Some of his friends may be his hidden enemies, and they may keep causing problems for him. In an extreme case, one or more of his good friends may die before native's age of 40 or 35.

The native may witness delays, financial losses, setbacks, failures, job loss, bad reputation and several other problems related to or through his profession. Taking an example, suppose combust Moon is placed in the ninth house of a horoscope in Taurus with malefic Sun and malefic Mars. Malefic Rahu is placed in the fourth house in Sagittarius, malefic Ketu is placed in the tenth house in Gemini with retrograde Venus; Mercury is placed in the eighth house in Aries with debilitated Saturn; and Jupiter is placed in the twelfth house in Leo.

In this case, native's mother may die before his age of 10 or 5. His father may get married again, but the native may not have a good equation with his stepmother. He may not find a permanent profession till his age of 35/40, or throughout his life, though he may earn well at times. He may remain jobless for periods of more than 3 months, many times in his life. He may lose one or more good friends to death, before his age of 35 or 30. He may not get married till his age of 35/40, or throughout his life.

Combust Moon in Ninth House in Gemini

When Sun and combust Moon are placed in the ninth house of a horoscope in Gemini, Libra rises in the ascendant. Sun rules the eleventh house, and Moon rules the tenth house. In general, this combination is benefic here, in most cases. The concept of various planets exhibiting tendencies to be benefic or malefic on the basis of the houses they rule in a horoscope has been explained in the book 'Gemstones: Magic or Science?'.

Combination of Sun and combust Moon in the ninth house of horoscope in Gemini is benefic in most cases, though it may turn malefic in some cases. It may happen when such combination is influenced by one or more malefic planets, and/or an overall malefic horoscope. The concept of a benefic planet turning malefic due to influences of malefic planets has been explained in the book 'Match Making and Manglik Dosh'.

When benefic in nature, combination of Sun and combust Moon in the ninth house of a horoscope in Gemini can bless the native with good results related to father, mother, creativity, spiritual growth, friends, profession, finances, reputation, authority, recognition, fame and several other good results, depending on his/her overall horoscope and running times.

Such combination of Sun and combust Moon can render various types of benefits to the native, related to or through his father, mother and/or friends. Considering parents, native's

father/mother may be a rich man/woman, a celebrity, an officer in government or a powerful politician. The native may enjoy many benefits because of his father/mother's money, influence and/or status. He/she may give a big amount of money, and/or wealth to the native, while he/she's alive, and/or through his/her will. Considering friends, some of his friends may stand by the native and they may help him get out of his problems, many times in his life. One or more of his friends may help him financially as well as in other ways, in order for him to start a new business, or repair/consolidate an already existing business.

Looking at profession, such combust Moon can help the native achieve success as a fire fighter, fitness trainer, body builder, sportsman, athlete, physician, dietician, lawyer, astrologer, tantric, psychic, spiritual guru, healer, religious guru, teacher, preacher, consultant, researcher, analyst, host, artist, poet, chef, interior designer, police officer, army, air force, naval, revenue, administrative, foreign services officer, judge, doctor, scientist, engineer, politician, professional dealing in education industry, coaching, food, health, pharma, medical, nursing, homecare, real estate, agriculture, hospitality, beauty, fashion, finance, television, music, sports, media, book, publishing, fitness, travel, hotel, airline, fishing, shipping, telecom, computer, software, IT, internet industry or some other type of professional, depending on his/her overall horoscope and running times.

Taking an example, suppose benefic combust Moon is placed in the ninth house of a horoscope in Gemini with benefic Sun. Mercury is placed in the tenth house in Cancer, Venus is placed in the eleventh house in Leo with Ketu; benefic

Rahu is placed in the fifth house in Aquarius, and benefic Mars is placed in the twelfth house in Virgo with Jupiter. In this case, the native may start a company which may manufacture various types of liquor products, and he may witness good results.

If benefic retrograde Saturn is placed in the second house in Scorpio, the equation may become better. In this case, the native may come across very good amount of success, money and recognition through liquor industry. His business may expand after his age of 35/40, and it may keep growing. If the finer factors and running times are supportive, he may own a business empire worth in billions, by his age of 55/60.

Such combust Moon can help the native achieve success through a creative field as an actor, singer, musician, writer, dancer, sportsman, artist, architect, designer, developer or some other likewise professional. Taking an example for a female native, suppose benefic combust Moon is placed in the ninth house of a horoscope in Gemini with Mercury and benefic Sun. Benefic debilitated Rahu is placed in the second house in Scorpio, Venus is placed in the eighth house in Taurus with debilitated Ketu; benefic Saturn is placed in the sixth house in Pisces, and retrograde Jupiter is placed in the fourth house in Capricorn. In this case, the native may become a fashion designer. She may start a company which may manufacture clothing and other fashion products. She may witness good results.

If benefic Mars is placed in the first house in Libra, the equation may become better. In this case, the native may come across very good amount of success, money and recognition through fashion industry, along with good amount of fame.

Her business may expand after her age of 35/40, and it may keep growing. If the finer factors and running times are supportive, she may own a business empire worth in billions, by her age of 50/55.

On the other hand, when malefic in nature, combination of Sun and combust Moon in the ninth house of a horoscope in Gemini can trouble the native with problems related to father, mother, friends, profession, finances, reputation, authority, recognition and several other problems, depending on his/her overall horoscope and running times.

Sun rules the eleventh house, Moon rules the tenth house, and they are placed in the ninth house. If such combination of Sun and combust Moon is influenced by malefic planets, and/or an overall malefic horoscope, the native may witness various types of problems related to or through his father, mother and/or friends. Considering parents, the native may not have a good equation with his father/mother, his parents may get divorced and he may live with his father/mother, his father/mother may suffer from a long-lasting illness, he/she may be an alcoholic and/or a drug addict, he/she may be a criminal, and/or he/she may die before native's age of 20, depending on native's overall horoscope and running times. Considering friends, some of his friends may be selfish, opportunists, criminal-minded, criminals, drug addicts, traitors and/or they may have some other negative traits. The native may witness several problems because of such friends, many times in his life. Some of his friends may be his hidden enemies, and they may keep causing problems for him. In an extreme case, one or more of his good friends may die before native's age of 40 or 35.

The native may witness delays, financial losses, setbacks, failures, job loss, bad reputation and several other problems related to or through his profession. Taking an example, suppose combust Moon is placed in the ninth house of a horoscope in Gemini with Sun, Mercury and malefic Ketu. Malefic Rahu is placed in the third house in Sagittarius, malefic retrograde Jupiter is placed in the twelfth house in Virgo with Saturn; Venus is placed in the eighth house in Taurus, and Mars is placed in the sixth house in Pisces. Grahan Yoga is formed in the ninth house.

In this case, native's mother may die before his age of 15 or 10. He may not have a good equation with his father. The native may not find a permanent profession throughout his life, and he may only find temporary jobs, though he may earn well at times. He may remain jobless for periods of more than 3 months, many times in his life. He may lose one or more good friends to death, before his age of 40 or 35. He may witness 1 or 2 failed marriages, and he may not get married after that.

Combust Moon in Ninth House in Cancer

When Sun and combust Moon are placed in the ninth house of a horoscope in Cancer, Scorpio rises in the ascendant. Sun rules the tenth house, and Moon rules the ninth house. In general, this combination is benefic here, in most cases. The concept of various planets exhibiting tendencies to be benefic or malefic on the basis of the houses they rule in a horoscope has been explained in the book 'Gemstones: Magic or Science?'.

Combination of Sun and combust Moon in the ninth house of horoscope in Cancer is benefic in most cases, though it may turn malefic in some cases. It may happen when such combination is influenced by one or more malefic planets, and/or an overall malefic horoscope. The concept of a benefic planet turning malefic due to influences of malefic planets has been explained in the book 'Match Making and Manglik Dosh'.

When benefic in nature, combination of Sun and combust Moon in the ninth house of a horoscope in Cancer can bless the native with good results related to father, mother, creativity, spiritual growth, profession, finances, reputation, authority, recognition, fame and several other good results, depending on his/her overall horoscope and running times.

Such combination of Sun and combust Moon can render various types of benefits to the native, related to or through his father and/or mother. Considering parents, native's father/mother may be a rich man/woman, a celebrity, an officer in government or a powerful politician. The native may enjoy many benefits because of his father/mother's money, influence and/or status. He/she may give a big amount of money, and/or wealth to the native, while he/she's alive, and/or through his/her will.

Looking at profession, such combust Moon can help the native achieve success as a fire fighter, fitness trainer, body builder, sportsman, athlete, physician, dietician, lawyer, astrologer, tantric, psychic, spiritual guru, healer, religious guru, teacher, preacher, consultant, researcher, analyst, host, artist, poet, chef, interior designer, professional dealing in education industry, coaching, food, health, pharma, medical, nursing, homecare, real estate, agriculture, hospitality, beauty, fashion, finance, television, music, sports, media, book, publishing, fitness, travel, hotel, airline, fishing, shipping, telecom, computer, software, IT, internet industry or some other type of professional, depending on his/her overall horoscope and running times.

Such combust Moon can help the native achieve success through a creative field as an actor, singer, musician, writer, dancer, sportsman, artist, architect, designer, developer or some other likewise professional. Taking an example, suppose benefic combust Moon is placed in the ninth house of a horoscope in Cancer with Mercury and benefic Sun. Venus is placed in the eighth house in Gemini, Mars is placed in the tenth house in Leo, benefic retrograde Saturn is placed in the second house in Sagittarius, benefic Rahu is placed in the sixth house in Aries, and Ketu is placed in the twelfth house in Libra. In this case, the native may become a singer, and he may witness good results.

If benefic Jupiter is placed in the seventh house in Taurus, the equation may become better. The native may possess remarkable singing talent, and he may come across very good amount of success, money, recognition and fame. He may deliver several hit songs, and he may receive many awards. If the finer factors and running times are supportive, he may become one of the greatest singers of all time, and his net worth may be in multimillions.

Such combust Moon can bless the native with authority in government as a police officer, army, air force, naval, revenue, administrative, foreign services officer, judge, doctor, scientist, engineer, politician or some other type of professional. Taking an example, suppose benefic combust Moon is placed in the ninth house of a horoscope in Cancer with Mars, Venus and benefic Sun. Benefic Jupiter is placed in the sixth house in Aries, Mercury is placed in the eighth house in Gemini, benefic debilitated Rahu is placed in the fifth house in Pisces, and debilitated Ketu is placed in the eleventh house in Virgo. In this case, the native may become an officer in police force, and he may enjoy a good career.

If benefic retrograde Saturn is placed in the first house in Scorpio, the equation may become better. In this case, the native may achieve success in civil exams, and he may get selected for the highest possible direct rank in police force. He may serve at several important posts during his career, and he may come across very good amount of success, recognition and authority. If the finer factors and running times are supportive, he may serve at one of the top 2 ranks in police force, before retirement.

On the other hand, when malefic in nature, combination of Sun and combust Moon in the ninth house of a horoscope in Cancer can trouble the native with problems related to father, mother, profession, finances, reputation, authority, recognition and several other problems, depending on his/her overall horoscope and running times.

Sun rules the tenth house, Moon rules the ninth house, and they are placed in the ninth house. If such combination of Sun and combust Moon is influenced by malefic planets, and/or an overall malefic horoscope, the native may witness various types of problems related to or through his father and/or mother. Considering parents, the native may not have a good equation with his father/mother, his parents may get divorced and he may live with his father/mother, his father/mother may suffer from a long-lasting illness, he/she may be an alcoholic and/or a drug addict, he/she may be a criminal, and/or he/she may die before native's age of 20, depending on native's overall horoscope and running times.

The native may witness delays, financial losses, setbacks, failures, job loss, bad reputation and several other problems related to or through his profession. Taking an example, suppose combust Moon is placed in the ninth house of a horoscope in Cancer with Sun, malefic Mercury and malefic Venus. Malefic Rahu is placed in the twelfth house in Libra, malefic Ketu is placed in the sixth house in Aries with retrograde Saturn; Jupiter is placed in the eighth house in Gemini, and Mars is placed in the seventh house in Taurus.

In this case, native's father as well as mother may die before his age of 15 or 10. He may not find a permanent profession throughout his life, and he may only find temporary jobs, though he may earn well at times. He may remain jobless for periods of more than 3 months, many times in his life. He may witness 1 or 2 failed marriages.

Combust Moon in Ninth House in Leo

When Sun and combust Moon are placed in the ninth house of a horoscope in Leo, Sagittarius rises in the ascendant. Sun rules the ninth house, and Moon rules the eighth house. In general, this combination is partly benefic and partly malefic here, though the benefic part is higher, in most cases. The concept of various planets exhibiting tendencies to be benefic or malefic on the basis of the houses they rule in a horoscope has been explained in the book 'Gemstones: Magic or Science?'.

Combination of Sun and combust Moon in the ninth house of horoscope in Leo is benefic in many cases, though it may turn malefic in some cases. It may happen when such combination is influenced by one or more malefic planets, and/or an overall malefic horoscope. The concept of a benefic planet turning malefic due to influences of malefic planets has been explained in the book 'Match Making and Manglik Dosh'.

When benefic in nature, combination of Sun and combust Moon in the ninth house of a horoscope in Leo can bless the native with good results related to father, mother, creativity, spiritual growth, profession, finances, reputation, authority, recognition, fame and several other good results, depending on his/her overall horoscope and running times.

Such combination of Sun and combust Moon can render various types of benefits to the native, related to or through

his father and/or mother. Considering parents, native's father/mother may be a rich man/woman, a celebrity, an officer in government or a powerful politician. The native may enjoy many benefits because of his father/mother's money, influence and/or status. He/she may give a big amount of money, and/or wealth to the native, while he/she's alive, and/or through his/her will.

Looking at profession, such combust Moon can help the native achieve success as a fire fighter, fitness trainer, body builder, sportsman, athlete, physician, dietician, lawyer, astrologer, tantric, psychic, spiritual guru, healer, religious guru, teacher, preacher, consultant, actor, singer, musician, writer, dancer, sportsman, artist, architect, designer, developer, poet, chef, interior designer, host, researcher, analyst, professional dealing in education industry, coaching, food, health, pharma, medical, nursing, homecare, real estate, agriculture, hospitality, beauty, fashion, finance, television, music, sports, media, book, publishing, fitness, travel, hotel, airline, fishing, shipping, telecom, computer, software, IT, internet industry or some other type of professional, depending on his/her overall horoscope and running times.

Taking an example, suppose combust Moon is placed in the ninth house of a horoscope in Leo with Ketu and benefic Sun. Benefic Rahu is placed in the third house in Aquarius, benefic Mercury is placed in the eighth house in Cancer, benefic retrograde Saturn is placed in the second house in Capricorn, and Mars is placed in the seventh house in Gemini with Venus. In this case, the native may become a journalist. He may get a well-paying job in a well-established newspaper, and he may witness good results.

If benefic Jupiter is placed in the ninth house in Leo with Sun, Moon and Ketu; the equation may become better. The native may possess remarkable talent, and he may come across very good amount of success and recognition, along with good amount of money and fame. He may engage in investigative journalism, and he may uncover several high-profile scandals and conspiracies. If the finer factors and running times are supportive, he may become one of the most recognized journalists of his time.

Such combust Moon can bless the native with authority in government as a police officer, army, air force, naval, revenue, administrative, foreign services officer, judge, doctor, scientist, engineer, politician or some other type of professional. Taking an example, suppose combust Moon is placed in the ninth house of a horoscope in Leo with Venus, benefic Mercury and benefic Sun. Benefic exalted Rahu is placed in the sixth house in Taurus with Mars; exalted Ketu is placed in the twelfth house in Scorpio, and benefic Saturn is placed in the eighth house in Cancer. Sun and Mercury form Budhaditya Yoga in the ninth house. In this case, the native may become an officer in army, and he may enjoy a good career.

If benefic retrograde Jupiter is placed in the seventh house in Gemini, the equation may become better. In this case, the native may achieve success in competitive exams, and he may get selected for the highest possible direct rank in army. He may serve at several important posts during his career, and he may come across very good amount of success, recognition and authority. If the finer factors and running times are supportive, he may serve at one of the top 2 ranks in army, before retirement.

On the other hand, when malefic in nature, combination of Sun and combust Moon in the ninth house of a horoscope in Leo can trouble the native with problems related to father, mother, lifespan, profession, finances, reputation, authority, recognition and several other problems, depending on his/her overall horoscope and running times.

Sun rules the ninth house, Moon rules the eighth house, and they are placed in the ninth house. If such combination of Sun and combust Moon is influenced by malefic planets, and/or an overall malefic horoscope, the native may witness various types of problems related to or through his father, mother and/or lifespan. Considering parents, the native may not have a good equation with his father/mother, his parents may get divorced and he may live with his father/mother, his father/mother may suffer from a long-lasting illness, he/she may be an alcoholic and/or a drug addict, he/she may be a criminal, and/or he/she may die before native's age of 20, depending on native's overall horoscope and running times. Considering lifespan, the native may witness reduction in lifespan due to several reasons. For example, the native may die in an accident, through a natural disaster, due to a fatal disease, due to a fatal viral infection like COVID, due to drug addiction, he may commit suicide, or someone may kill him intentionally or unintentionally. Considering some unintentional incidents, he may get caught in a crossfire between two rival criminal gangs or that between criminals and police, or someone may accidently kill him.

The native may witness delays, financial losses, setbacks, failures, job loss, bad reputation and several other problems related to or through his profession. Taking an example, suppose malefic combust Moon is placed in the ninth house of a horoscope in Leo with Sun, Mars and malefic Rahu. Malefic Ketu is placed in the third house in Aquarius with retrograde Saturn; Jupiter is placed in the twelfth house in Scorpio, Mercury is placed in the eighth house in Cancer, and malefic Venus is placed in the seventh house in Gemini. Grahan Yoga and Angarak Yoga are formed in the ninth house.

In this case, native's father may die before native's age of 10 or 5. His mother may ger married again, but the native may not have a good equation with his stepfather. His mother may also die before native's age of 25 or 20. He may not find a permanent profession throughout his life, and he may keep losing jobs, though he may earn well at times. He may remain jobless for periods of more than 3 months, many times in his life. He may witness 1 or 2 failed marriages. He may die before his age of 60 or 55, due to a heart attack, in an accident, due to a fatal disease like Cancer, or because of a fatal viral infection like COVID.

Combust Moon in Ninth House in Virgo

When Sun and combust Moon are placed in the ninth house of a horoscope in Virgo, Capricorn rises in the ascendant. Sun rules the eighth house, and Moon rules the seventh house. In general, this combination is partly benefic and partly malefic here, though the benefic part is higher, in most cases. The concept of various planets exhibiting tendencies to be benefic or malefic on the basis of the houses they rule in a horoscope has been explained in the book 'Gemstones: Magic or Science?'.

Combination of Sun and combust Moon in the ninth house of horoscope in Virgo is benefic in many cases, though it may turn malefic in some cases. It may happen when such combination is influenced by one or more malefic planets, and/or an overall malefic horoscope. The concept of a benefic planet turning malefic due to influences of malefic planets has been explained in the book 'Match Making and Manglik Dosh'.

When benefic in nature, combination of Sun and combust Moon in the ninth house of a horoscope in Virgo can bless the native with good results related to father, mother, creativity, spiritual growth, marriage, husband, wife, profession, finances, reputation, authority, recognition, fame and several other good results, depending on his/her overall horoscope and running times.

Such combination of Sun and combust Moon can render various types of benefits to the native, related to or through his father, mother and/or marriage. Considering parents, native's

father/mother may be a rich man/woman, a celebrity, an officer in government or a powerful politician. The native may enjoy many benefits because of his father/mother's money, influence and/or status. He/she may give a big amount of money, and/or wealth to the native, while he/she's alive, and/or through his/her will. Considering marriage, the native may get married to a woman who may be beautiful, rich, a celebrity, an officer in government, a powerful politician, a successful businesswoman, and/or a citizen of a foreign country. The native may witness several benefits due to or through his wife and/or her family members.

Looking at profession, such combust Moon can help the native achieve success as a fire fighter, fitness trainer, body builder, sportsman, athlete, physician, dietician, lawyer, astrologer, tantric, psychic, spiritual guru, healer, religious guru, teacher, preacher, consultant, researcher, analyst, host, artist, poet, chef, interior designer, professional dealing in education industry, coaching, food, health, pharma, medical, nursing, homecare, real estate, agriculture, hospitality, beauty, fashion, finance, television, music, sports, media, book, publishing, fitness, travel, hotel, airline, fishing, shipping, telecom, computer, software, IT, internet industry or some other type of professional, depending on his/her overall horoscope and running times.

Such combust Moon can help the native achieve success through a creative field as an actor, singer, musician, writer, dancer, sportsman, artist, architect, designer, developer or some other likewise professional. Taking an example, suppose benefic combust Moon is placed in the ninth house of a horoscope in Virgo with Sun, exalted Mercury and benefic debilitated Venus. Benefic Saturn is placed in the third house in Pisces, benefic Rahu is placed in the second house in Aquarius, Ketu is placed in the eighth house in Leo, and Jupiter is placed in the fourth house in Aries. In this case, the native may become a movie director, and he may witness good results.

If benefic retrograde Mars is placed in the eleventh house in Scorpio, the equation may become better. The native may possess remarkable talent, and he may come across very good amount of success, money, recognition and fame. He may deliver several hit movies, and he may receive many awards. If the finer factors and running times are supportive, he may become one of the most successful movie directors of his time, and his net worth may be in multimillions.

Such combust Moon can bless the native with authority in government as a police officer, army, air force, naval, revenue, administrative, foreign services officer, judge, doctor, scientist, engineer, politician or some other type of professional. Taking an example, suppose benefic combust Moon is placed in the ninth house of a horoscope in Virgo with Sun and benefic debilitated Venus. Mercury is placed in the tenth house in Libra, benefic Mars is placed in the third house in Pisces, benefic Rahu is placed in the first house in Capricorn, Ketu is placed in the seventh house in Cancer, and Jupiter is placed in the eighth house in Leo. In this case, the native may engage in politics, and he may become a minister in a state government.

If benefic Saturn is placed in the ninth house in Virgo with Sun, Moon and Venus, the equation may become better. In this case, the native may come across very good amount of success, recognition, authority and fame through politics. He may win several elections, and he may become chief minister or governor of a state. If the finer factors and running times are supportive, he may hold one such post, more than once in his life.

On the other hand, when malefic in nature, combination of Sun and combust Moon in the ninth house of a horoscope in Virgo can trouble the native with problems related to father, mother, marriage, husband, wife, lifespan, profession, finances, reputation, authority, recognition and several other problems, depending on his/her overall horoscope and running times.

Sun rules the eighth house, Moon rules the seventh house, and they are placed in the ninth house. If such combination of Sun and combust Moon is influenced by malefic planets, and/or an overall malefic horoscope, the native may witness various types of problems related to or through his father, mother, marriage and/or lifespan. Considering parents, the native may not have a good equation with his father/mother, his parents may get divorced and he may live with his father/mother, his father/mother may suffer from a long-lasting illness, he/she may be an alcoholic and/or a drug addict, he/she may be a criminal, and/or he/she may die before native's age of 20, depending on native's overall horoscope and running times. Considering marriage, the native may witness delay/disturbances in marriage, and/or one or more failed marriages. He may have serious differences of opinion with his wife, she may suffer from a long-lasting illness, she may be an alcoholic and/or a drug addict, she may be a criminal, she may not be loyal to him, she may have extramarital affair/affairs, and/or she may die within 10 or 5 years of marriage. Considering lifespan, the native may witness reduction in lifespan due to several reasons. For example, the native may die in an accident, through a natural disaster, due to a fatal disease, due to a fatal viral infection like COVID, due to drug addiction, he may commit suicide, or someone may kill him intentionally or unintentionally. Considering some unintentional incidents, he may get caught in a crossfire between two rival criminal gangs or that between criminals and police, or someone may accidently kill him.

The native may witness delays, financial losses, setbacks, failures, job loss, bad reputation and several other problems related to or through his profession. Taking an example, suppose combust Moon is placed in the ninth house of a horoscope in Virgo with exalted Mercury, malefic Sun and malefic exalted Rahu. Malefic exalted Ketu is placed in the third house in Pisces with malefic Jupiter; Venus is placed in the eighth house in Leo, Mars is placed in the twelfth house in Sagittarius, and retrograde Saturn is placed in the sixth house in Gemini. Grahan Yoga is formed in the ninth house whereas Guru Chandal Yoga is formed in the third house.

In this case, native's mother may die before his age of 10 or 5. His father may get married again, but the native may not have a good equation with his stepmother. He may not find a permanent profession till his age of 35/40, or throughout his life, though he may earn well at times. He may witness financial tightness and debts from time to time. He may witness 1 or 2 failed marriages. He my die before his age of 60 or 55, due to a heart attack, some type of cancer, or another fatal disease.

Combust Moon in Ninth House in Libra

When Sun and combust Moon are placed in the ninth house of a horoscope in Libra, Aquarius rises in the ascendant. Sun rules the seventh house, and Moon rules the sixth house. In general, this combination is partly benefic and partly malefic here, though the malefic part is higher, in most cases. The concept of various planets exhibiting tendencies to be benefic or malefic on the basis of the houses they rule in a horoscope has been explained in the book 'Gemstones: Magic or Science?'.

Combination of Sun and combust Moon in the ninth house of horoscope in Libra is malefic in many cases, though it may turn benefic in some cases. It may happen when such combination is influenced by one or more benefic planets, and/or an overall benefic horoscope. The concept of a malefic planet turning benefic due to influences of benefic planets has been explained in the book 'Match Making and Manglik Dosh'.

When benefic in nature, combination of Sun and combust Moon in the ninth house of a horoscope in Libra can bless the native with good results related to father, mother, creativity, spiritual growth, marriage, husband, wife, profession, finances, reputation, authority, recognition, fame and several other good results, depending on his/her overall horoscope and running times.

Such combination of Sun and combust Moon can render various types of benefits to the native, related to or through his father, mother and/or marriage. Considering parents, native's

father/mother may be a rich man/woman, a celebrity, an officer in government or a powerful politician. The native may enjoy many benefits because of his father/mother's money, influence and/or status. He/she may give a big amount of money, and/or wealth to the native, while he/she's alive, and/ or through his/her will. Considering marriage, the native may get married to a woman who may be beautiful, rich, a celebrity, an officer in government, a powerful politician, a successful businesswoman, and/or a citizen of a foreign country. The native may witness several benefits due to or through his wife and/or her family members.

Looking at profession, such combust Moon can help the native achieve success as a fire fighter, fitness trainer, body builder, sportsman, athlete, physician, dietician, lawyer, astrologer, tantric, psychic, spiritual guru, healer, religious guru, teacher, preacher, consultant, researcher, analyst, host, artist, poet, chef, interior designer, professional dealing in education industry, coaching, food, health, pharma, medical, nursing, homecare, real estate, agriculture, hospitality, beauty, fashion, finance, television, music, sports, media, book, publishing, fitness, travel, hotel, airline, fishing, shipping, telecom, computer, software, IT, internet industry or some other type of professional, depending on his/her overall horoscope and running times.

Such combust Moon can help the native achieve success through a creative field as an actor, singer, musician, writer, dancer, sportsman, artist, architect, designer, developer or some other likewise professional. Taking an example, suppose combust Moon is placed in the ninth house of a horoscope in Libra with Mercury, benefic Venus and benefic debilitated

Sun. Benefic retrograde Jupiter is placed in the third house in Aries with debilitated Saturn; benefic Rahu is placed in the fifth house in Gemini, and Ketu is placed in the eleventh house in Sagittarius. Sun and Venus form Neechbhang Rajyoga in the ninth house. In this case, the native may write fictional books, and he may witness good results.

If benefic Mars is placed in eighth house in Virgo, the equation may become better. The native may possess remarkable writing talent, and he may come across very good amount of success, money, recognition and fame. He may write in several genres, including action, crime, science-fiction and fantasy. He may deliver several bestsellers, and he may receive many awards. If the finer factors and running times are supportive, he may become one of the most successful writers of his time, and his net worth may be in multimillions.

Such combust Moon can bless the native with authority in government as a police officer, army, air force, naval, revenue, administrative, foreign services officer, judge, doctor, scientist, engineer, politician or some other type of professional. Taking an example, suppose combust Moon is placed in the ninth house of a horoscope in Libra with Mercury, exalted Saturn and benefic debilitated Sun. Benefic Jupiter is placed in the seventh house in Leo, benefic Rahu is placed in the sixth house in Cancer, Ketu is placed in the twelfth house in Capricorn, and benefic Mars is placed in the first house in Aquarius. In this case, the native may become an officer in administrative services, and he may enjoy a good career.

If benefic Venus is placed in the ninth house in Libra with Sun, Moon, Mercury and Saturn; the equation may become better. Sun and Venus form Neechbhang Rajyoga in the ninth house. In this case, the native may achieve success in civil exams, and he may get selected for the highest possible direct rank in administrative services. He may serve at several important posts during his career, and he may come across very good amount of success, recognition and authority. If the finer factors and running times are supportive, he may serve as the head of an administrative department, before retirement.

On the other hand, when malefic in nature, combination of Sun and combust Moon in the ninth house of a horoscope in Libra can trouble the native with problems related to father, mother, marriage, husband, wife, profession, finances, reputation, authority, recognition and several other problems, depending on his/her overall horoscope and running times.

Sun rules the seventh house, Moon rules the sixth house, and they are placed in the ninth house. If such combination of Sun and combust Moon is influenced by malefic planets, and/or an overall malefic horoscope, the native may witness various types of problems related to or through his father, mother and/or marriage. Considering parents, the native may not have a good equation with his father/mother, his parents may get divorced and he may live with his father/mother, his father/mother may suffer from a long-lasting illness, he/she may be an alcoholic and/or a drug addict, he/she may be a criminal, and/or he/she may die before native's age of 20, depending on native's overall horoscope and running times. Considering marriage, the native may witness delay/disturbances in marriage, and/or one or more failed marriages. He may have serious differences of opinion with his wife, she may suffer from a long-lasting illness, she may be an alcoholic and/or a drug addict, she may be a criminal, she may not be loyal to him, she may have extramarital affair/affairs, and/or she may die within 10 or 5 years of marriage.

The native may witness delays, financial losses, setbacks, failures, job loss, bad reputation and several other problems related to or through his profession. Taking an example, suppose malefic combust Moon is placed in the ninth house of a horoscope in Libra with Venus, debilitated Sun and malefic Rahu. Malefic Ketu is placed in the third house in Aries, retrograde Saturn is placed in the fourth house in Taurus, Mercury is placed in the tenth house in Scorpio, debilitated Mars is placed in the sixth house in Cancer, and debilitated Jupiter is placed in the twelfth house in Capricorn. Grahan Yoga is formed in the ninth house.

In this case, native's mother may die before his age of 15 or 10. His father may get married again, but the native may not have a good equation with his stepmother. He may not find a permanent profession throughout his life, and he may keep losing jobs. He may remain jobless for periods of more than 3 months, many times in his life. He may witness 1 or 2 failed marriages, and he may settle in his second or third marriage.

Combust Moon in Ninth House in Scorpio

When Sun and combust Moon are placed in the ninth house of a horoscope in Scorpio, Pisces rises in the ascendant. Sun rules the sixth house, and Moon rules the fifth house. In general, this combination is partly benefic and partly malefic here, though the benefic part is higher, in most cases. The concept of various planets exhibiting tendencies to be benefic or malefic on the basis of the houses they rule in a horoscope has been explained in the book 'Gemstones: Magic or Science?'.

Combination of Sun and combust Moon in the ninth house of horoscope in Scorpio is benefic in many cases, though it may turn malefic in some cases. It may happen when such combination is influenced by one or more malefic planets, and/or an overall malefic horoscope. The concept of a benefic planet turning malefic due to influences of malefic planets has been explained in the book 'Match Making and Manglik Dosh'.

When benefic in nature, combination of Sun and combust Moon in the ninth house of a horoscope in Scorpio can bless the native with good results related to father, mother, creativity, spiritual growth, love life, children, profession, finances, reputation, authority, recognition, fame and several other good results, depending on his/her overall horoscope and running times.

Such combination of Sun and combust Moon can render various types of benefits to the native, related to or through

his father, mother and/or children. Considering parents, native's father/mother may be a rich man/woman, a celebrity, an officer in government or a powerful politician. The native may enjoy many benefits because of his father/mother's money, influence and/or status. He/she may give a big amount of money, and/or wealth to the native, while he/she's alive, and/or through his/her will. Considering children, the native may have children who may be physically, intellectually, emotionally, creatively and/or spiritually better or much better than average. Such children may achieve a lot in many spheres of their lives, and they may bring good name and many other good results to the native.

Looking at profession, such combust Moon can help the native achieve success as a fire fighter, fitness trainer, body builder, sportsman, athlete, physician, dietician, lawyer, astrologer, tantric, psychic, spiritual guru, healer, religious guru, teacher, preacher, consultant, researcher, analyst, host, artist, poet, chef, interior designer, professional dealing in education industry, coaching, food, health, pharma, medical, nursing, homecare, real estate, agriculture, hospitality, beauty, fashion, finance, television, music, sports, media, book, publishing, fitness, travel, hotel, airline, fishing, shipping, telecom, computer, software, IT, internet industry or some other type of professional, depending on his/her overall horoscope and running times.

Such combust Moon can help the native achieve success through a creative field as an actor, singer, musician, writer, dancer, sportsman, artist, architect, designer, developer or some other likewise professional. Taking an example, suppose benefic combust Moon is placed in the ninth house of a horoscope in Scorpio with Sun, Venus and benefic Mercury. Benefic retrograde Jupiter is placed in the second house in Aries with benefic Rahu; Ketu is placed in the eighth house in Libra, and Saturn is placed in the seventh house in Virgo. In this case, the native may become an actor, and he may witness good results.

If benefic debilitated Mars is placed in the fifth house in Cancer, the equation may become better. The native may possess remarkable acting talent, and he may come across very good amount of success, money, recognition and fame. He may perform very well in the genres of drama, action and romance. He may deliver several hit movies, and he may receive many awards. If the finer factors and running times are supportive, he may become one of the most successful actors of his time, and his net worth may be in multimillions.

Such combust Moon can bless the native with authority in government as a police officer, army, air force, naval, revenue, administrative, foreign services officer, judge, doctor, scientist, engineer, politician or some other type of professional. Taking an example, suppose benefic combust Moon is placed in the ninth house of a horoscope in Scorpio with Sun and benefic retrograde Mercury. Benefic Mars is placed in the eighth house in Libra with benefic Rahu; Ketu is placed in the second house in Aries, retrograde Venus is placed in the tenth house in Sagittarius, and Saturn is placed in the sixth house in Leo. In this case, the native may become an officer in revenue services, and he may enjoy a good career.

If benefic Jupiter is placed in the ninth house in Scorpio with Sun, Moon and Mercury; the equation may become better. Moon and Jupiter form Gaj Kesari Yoga in the ninth house.

In this case, the native may achieve success in civil exams, and he may get selected for the highest possible direct rank in revenue services. He may serve at several important posts during his career, and he may come across very good amount of success, recognition and authority. If the finer factors and running times are supportive, he may serve as the head of a revenue department, before retirement.

On the other hand, when malefic in nature, combination of Sun and combust Moon in the ninth house of a horoscope in Scorpio can trouble the native with problems related to father, mother, love life, children, profession, finances, reputation, authority, recognition and several other problems, depending on his/her overall horoscope and running times.

Sun rules the sixth house, Moon rules the fifth house, and they are placed in the ninth house. If such combination of Sun and combust Moon is influenced by malefic planets, and/or an overall malefic horoscope, the native may witness various types of problems related to or through his father, mother and/or children. Considering parents, the native may not have a good equation with his father/mother, his parents may get divorced and he may live with his father/mother, his father/mother may suffer from a long-lasting illness, he/she may be an alcoholic and/or a drug addict, he/she may be a criminal, and/or he/she may die before native's age of 20, depending on native's overall horoscope and running times. Considering children, the native may lose one or more children through miscarriages that his wife may witness. He may witness delay in childbirth, and/or he may have children who may be physically and/or mentally troubled in some way. He may lose his children through divorce, or his children may engage in immoral/illegal activities, and he may witness bad reputation and many other problems because of them. In an extreme case, the native may witness death of one or more children during their young ages.

The native may witness delays, financial losses, setbacks, failures, job loss, bad reputation and several other problems related to or through his profession. Taking an example, suppose combust Moon is placed in the ninth house of a horoscope in Scorpio with Mercury, malefic Sun and malefic Venus. Malefic Rahu is placed in the fourth house in Gemini, malefic Ketu is placed in the tenth house in Sagittarius with malefic Saturn; benefic Jupiter is placed in the seventh house in Virgo, and Mars is placed in the twelfth house in Aquarius.

In this case, native's mother may die before his age of 10 or 5. His father may get married again, but the native may not have a good equation with his stepmother. He may not find a permanent profession till his age of 35/40, or throughout his life, and he may only find temporary jobs. He may remain jobless for periods of more than 6 months, many times in his life. He may witness 1 or 2 failed marriages. He may lose one or more children to death, through miscarriages that his wife/wives may witness.

Combust Moon in Ninth House in Sagittarius

When Sun and combust Moon are placed in the ninth house of a horoscope in Sagittarius, Aries rises in the ascendant. Sun rules the fifth house, and Moon rules the fourth house. In general, this combination is benefic here, in most cases. The concept of various planets exhibiting tendencies to be benefic or malefic on the basis of the houses they rule in a horoscope has been explained in the book 'Gemstones: Magic or Science?'.

Combination of Sun and combust Moon in the ninth house of horoscope in Sagittarius is benefic in most cases, though it may turn malefic in some cases. It may happen when such combination is influenced by one or more malefic planets, and/or an overall malefic horoscope. The concept of a benefic planet turning malefic due to influences of malefic planets has been explained in the book 'Match Making and Manglik Dosh'.

When benefic in nature, combination of Sun and combust Moon in the ninth house of a horoscope in Sagittarius can bless the native with good results related to father, mother, creativity, spiritual growth, education, wealth, properties, vehicles, love life, children, profession, finances, reputation, authority, recognition, fame and several other good results, depending on his/her overall horoscope and running times.

Such combination of Sun and combust Moon can render various types of benefits to the native, related to or through his

father, mother and/or children. Considering parents, native's father/mother may be a rich man/woman, a celebrity, an officer in government or a powerful politician. The native may enjoy many benefits because of his father/mother's money, influence and/or status. He/she may give a big amount of money, and/or wealth to the native, while he/she's alive, and/or through his/her will. This combination can bless the native with good education, vehicles, residential house/houses and/or several other good results. Considering children, the native may have children who may be physically, intellectually, emotionally, creatively and/or spiritually better or much better than average. Such children may achieve a lot in many spheres of their lives, and they may bring good name and many other good results to the native.

Looking at profession, such combust Moon can help the native achieve success as a fire fighter, fitness trainer, body builder, sportsman, athlete, physician, dietician, lawyer, astrologer, tantric, psychic, spiritual guru, healer, religious guru, teacher, preacher, consultant, researcher, analyst, host, artist, poet, chef, interior designer, professional dealing in education industry, coaching, food, health, pharma, medical, nursing, homecare, real estate, agriculture, hospitality, beauty, fashion, finance, television, music, sports, media, book, publishing, fitness, travel, hotel, airline, fishing, shipping, telecom, computer, software, IT, internet industry or some other type of professional, depending on his/her overall horoscope and running times.

Such combust Moon can help the native achieve success as an actor, singer, musician, writer, dancer, sportsman, artist, architect, designer, developer or some other likewise professional. Taking an example, suppose benefic combust Moon is placed in the ninth house of a horoscope in Sagittarius with Mercury and benefic Sun. Benefic retrograde Saturn is placed in the third house in Gemini, benefic Rahu is placed in the first house in Aries, Ketu is placed in the seventh house in Libra, Mars is placed in the sixth house in Virgo, and Jupiter is placed in the fifth house in Leo. In this case, the native may become a professional footballer, and he may witness good results.

If benefic Venus is placed in the ninth house in Sagittarius with Sun, Moon and Mercury; the equation may become better. The native may possess remarkable talent related to the sport, and he may come across very good amount of success, money, recognition and fame. He may deliver several match-winning performances, and he may receive many awards/ medals. If the finer factors and running times are supportive, he may become one of the most successful footballers of his time, and his net worth may be in multimillions.

Such combust Moon can bless the native with authority in government as a police officer, army, air force, naval, revenue, administrative, foreign services officer, judge, doctor, scientist, engineer, politician or some other type of professional. Taking an example, suppose benefic combust Moon is placed in the ninth house of a horoscope in Sagittarius with benefic Sun. Benefic Venus is placed in the eighth house in Scorpio with Mercury and exalted Ketu; benefic exalted Rahu is placed in the second house in Taurus, benefic Saturn is placed in the eleventh house in Aquarius, and Mars is placed in the sixth house in Virgo. In this case, the native may become an officer in police force, and he may enjoy a good career.

If retrograde Jupiter is placed in the first house in Aries, the equation may become better. In this case, the native may achieve success in civil exams, and he may get selected for the highest possible direct rank in police force. He may serve at several important posts during his career, and he may come across very good amount of success, recognition and authority. If the finer factors and running times are supportive, he may serve at one of the top 2 ranks in police force, before retirement.

On the other hand, when malefic in nature, combination of Sun and combust Moon in the ninth house of a horoscope in Sagittarius can trouble the native with problems related to father, mother, education, wealth, properties, vehicles, love life, children, profession, finances, reputation, authority, recognition and several other problems, depending on his/her overall horoscope and running times.

Sun rules the fifth house, Moon rules the fourth house, and they are placed in the ninth house. If such combination of Sun and combust Moon is influenced by malefic planets, and/or an overall malefic horoscope, the native may witness various types of problems related to or through his father, mother and/or children. Considering parents, the native may not have a good equation with his father/mother, his parents may get divorced and he may live with his father/mother, his father/mother may suffer from a long-lasting illness, he/she may be an alcoholic and/or a drug addict, he/she may be a criminal, and/or he/she may die before native's age of 20, depending on native's overall horoscope and running times. He may also witness various types of problems related to properties, vehicles and/or mental health. Considering children, the native may lose one or more children through miscarriages that his wife may witness. He may witness delay in childbirth, and/or he may have children who may be physically and/or mentally troubled in some way. He may lose his children through divorce, or his children may engage in immoral/illegal activities, and he may witness bad reputation and many other problems because of them. In an extreme case, the native may witness death of one or more children during their young ages.

The native may witness delays, financial losses, setbacks, failures, job loss, bad reputation and several other problems related to or through his profession. Taking an example, suppose combust Moon is placed in the ninth house of a horoscope in Sagittarius with Sun, retrograde Venus and malefic Mercury. Malefic Rahu is placed in the fourth house in Cancer with exalted Jupiter; malefic Ketu is placed in the tenth house in Capricorn, retrograde Mars is placed in the fifth house in Leo, and Saturn is placed in the eighth house in Scorpio.

In this case, native's mother may die before his age of 15 or 10. His father may get married again, but the native may not have a good equation with his stepmother. He may not find a permanent profession till his age of 35/40, or throughout his life, though he may earn well at times. He may remain jobless for periods of more than 3 months, many times in his life. He may witness 1 or 2 failed marriages. He may lose one or more children to death, through miscarriages that his wife/wives may witness.

Combust Moon in Ninth House in Capricorn

When Sun and combust Moon are placed in the ninth house of a horoscope in Capricorn, Taurus rises in the ascendant. Sun rules the fourth house, and Moon rules the third house. In general, this combination is benefic here, in most cases. The concept of various planets exhibiting tendencies to be benefic or malefic on the basis of the houses they rule in a horoscope has been explained in the book 'Gemstones: Magic or Science?'.

Combination of Sun and combust Moon in the ninth house of horoscope in Capricorn is benefic in most cases, though it may turn malefic in some cases. It may happen when such combination is influenced by one or more malefic planets, and/or an overall malefic horoscope. The concept of a benefic planet turning malefic due to influences of malefic planets has been explained in the book 'Match Making and Manglik Dosh'.

When benefic in nature, combination of Sun and combust Moon in the ninth house of a horoscope in Capricorn can bless the native with good results related to father, mother, creativity, spiritual growth, education, wealth, properties, vehicles, siblings, colleagues, profession, finances, reputation, authority, recognition, fame and several other good results, depending on his/her overall horoscope and running times.

Such combination of Sun and combust Moon can render various types of benefits to the native, related to or through his father, mother and/or siblings. Considering parents, native's father/mother may be a rich man/woman, a celebrity, an officer in government or a powerful politician. The native may enjoy many benefits because of his father/mother's money, influence and/or status. He/she may give a big amount of money, and/or wealth to the native, while he/she's alive, and/ or through his/her will. This combination can bless the native with good education, vehicles, residential house/houses and/ or several other good results. Considering siblings, some of them may stand by the native and they may help him get out of his problems, many times in his life. A sibling of the native may give him a big amount of money, and/or wealth, while such sibling is alive, and/or through his/her will.

Looking at profession, such combust Moon can help the native achieve success as a fire fighter, fitness trainer, body builder, sportsman, athlete, physician, dietician, lawyer, astrologer, tantric, psychic, spiritual guru, healer, religious guru, teacher, preacher, consultant, researcher, analyst, host, artist, poet, chef, interior designer, professional dealing in education industry, coaching, food, health, pharma, medical, nursing, homecare, real estate, agriculture, hospitality, beauty, fashion, finance, television, music, sports, media, book, publishing, fitness, travel, hotel, airline, fishing, shipping, telecom, computer, software, IT, internet industry or some other type of professional, depending on his/her overall horoscope and running times.

Such combust Moon can help the native achieve success through a creative field as an actor, singer, musician, writer, dancer, sportsman, artist, architect, designer, developer or some other likewise professional. Taking an example, suppose benefic combust Moon is placed in the ninth house of a horoscope in Capricorn with benefic Sun and benefic

Mercury. Venus is placed in the eighth house in Sagittarius, benefic exalted Rahu is placed in the fifth house in Virgo, exalted Ketu is placed in the eleventh house in Pisces with retrograde Jupiter; and Mars is placed in the fourth house in Leo. Sun and Mercury form Budhaditya Yoga in the ninth house. In this case, the native may write fictional books, and he may witness good results.

If benefic Saturn is placed in the second house in Gemini, the equation may become better. The native may possess remarkable writing talent, and he may come across very good amount of success, money, recognition and fame. He may write in several genres, in fiction as well as non-fiction. He may deliver several bestsellers, and he may receive many awards. If the finer factors and running times are supportive, he may become one of the most successful writers of his time, and his net worth may be in multimillions.

Such combust Moon can bless the native with authority in government as a police officer, army, air force, naval, revenue, administrative, foreign services officer, judge, doctor, scientist, engineer, politician or some other type of professional. Taking an example, suppose benefic combust Moon is placed in the ninth house of a horoscope in Capricorn with Venus and benefic Sun. Benefic Mercury is placed in the eighth house in Sagittarius, benefic Rahu is placed in the tenth house in Aquarius with retrograde Jupiter; Ketu is placed in the fourth house in Leo, and Mars is placed in the seventh house in Scorpio. In this case, the native may engage in politics, and he may become a member of parliament of his country.

If benefic Saturn is placed in the first house in Taurus, the equation may become better. In this case, the native may come across very good amount of success, recognition, authority and fame through politics. He may win several elections, and he may become a minister in national government. If the finer factors and running times are supportive, he may serve as prime minister or president of his country.

On the other hand, when malefic in nature, combination of Sun and combust Moon in the ninth house of a horoscope in Capricorn can trouble the native with problems related to father, mother, education, wealth, properties, vehicles, siblings, colleagues, profession, finances, reputation, authority, recognition and several other problems, depending on his/her overall horoscope and running times.

Sun rules the fourth house, Moon rules the third house, and they are placed in the ninth house. If such combination of Sun and combust Moon is influenced by malefic planets, and/or an overall malefic horoscope, the native may witness various types of problems related to or through his father, mother and/or siblings. Considering parents, the native may not have a good equation with his father/mother, his parents may get divorced and he may live with his father/mother, his father/mother may suffer from a long-lasting illness, he/she may be an alcoholic and/or a drug addict, he/she may be a criminal, .and/or he/she may die before native's age of 20, depending on native's overall horoscope and running times. He may also witness various types of problems related to properties, vehicles and/or mental health. Considering siblings, the native may have bad relationships with some of his siblings, and/or he may witness various types of problems through them or due to them. The native may have siblings who may be criminals, and/or drug addicts, and he may face several problems because of them. In an extreme case, the native may lose one or more siblings to death, before his age of 40 or 35.

The native may witness delays, financial losses, setbacks, failures, job loss, bad reputation and several other problems related to or through his profession. Taking an example, suppose combust Moon is placed in the ninth house of a horoscope in Capricorn with Sun, malefic debilitated Jupiter and malefic exalted Mars. Mercury is placed in the eighth house in Sagittarius, Venus is placed in the seventh house in Scorpio, malefic Rahu is placed in the sixth house in Libra, and malefic Ketu is placed in the twelfth house in Aries with debilitated Saturn.

In this case, native's father as well as mother may die before his age of 15 or 10. He may witness a troublesome childhood. He may not find a permanent profession till his age of 35/40, or throughout his life. He may remain jobless for periods of more than 6 months, many times in his life. He may lose one or more siblings to death, before his age of 35 or 30. He may witness 1 or 2 failed marriages.

Combust Moon in Ninth House in Aquarius

When Sun and combust Moon are placed in the ninth house of a horoscope in Aquarius, Gemini rises in the ascendant. Sun rules the third house, and Moon rules the second house. In general, this combination is benefic here, in most cases. The concept of various planets exhibiting tendencies to be benefic or malefic on the basis of the houses they rule in a horoscope has been explained in the book 'Gemstones: Magic or Science?'.

Combination of Sun and combust Moon in the ninth house of horoscope in Aquarius is benefic in most cases, though it may turn malefic in some cases. It may happen when such combination is influenced by one or more malefic planets, and/or an overall malefic horoscope. The concept of a benefic planet turning malefic due to influences of malefic planets has been explained in the book 'Match Making and Manglik Dosh'.

When benefic in nature, combination of Sun and combust Moon in the ninth house of a horoscope in Aquarius can bless the native with good results related to father, mother, creativity, spiritual growth, family, wealth, speech, siblings, colleagues, profession, finances, reputation, authority, recognition, fame and several other good results, depending on his/her overall horoscope and running times.

Such combination of Sun and combust Moon can render various types of benefits to the native, related to or through

his father, mother, family and/or siblings. Considering parents, native's father/mother may be a rich man/woman, a celebrity, an officer in government or a powerful politician. The native may enjoy many benefits because of his father/mother's money, influence and/or status. He/she may give a big amount of money, and/or wealth to the native, while he/she's alive, and/or through his/her will. Considering siblings, some of them may stand by the native and they may help him get out of his problems, many times in his life. A sibling of the native may give him a big amount of money, and/or wealth, while such sibling is alive, and/or through his/her will.

Looking at profession, such combust Moon can help the native achieve success as a fire fighter, fitness trainer, body builder, sportsman, athlete, physician, dietician, lawyer, astrologer, tantric, psychic, spiritual guru, healer, religious guru, teacher, preacher, consultant, researcher, analyst, host, artist, poet, chef, interior designer, police officer, army, air force, naval, revenue, administrative, foreign services officer, judge, doctor, scientist, engineer, politician, professional dealing in education industry, coaching, food, health, pharma, medical, nursing, homecare, real estate, agriculture, hospitality, beauty, fashion, finance, television, music, sports, media, book, publishing, fitness, travel, hotel, airline, fishing, shipping, telecom, computer, software, IT, internet industry or some other type of professional, depending on his/her overall horoscope and running times.

Such combust Moon can help the native achieve success through a creative field as an actor, singer, musician, writer, dancer, sportsman, artist, architect, designer, developer or some other likewise professional. Taking an example, suppose benefic combust Moon is placed in the ninth house of a horoscope in Aquarius with benefic Sun and benefic Mercury. Exalted Venus is placed in the tenth house in Pisces, benefic Rahu is placed in the eleventh house in Aries, Ketu is placed in the fifth house in Libra with Mars; and Saturn is placed in the seventh house in Sagittarius. Sun and Mercury form Budhaditya Yoga in the ninth house. In this case, the native may become a singer, and he may witness good results.

If benefic retrograde Jupiter is placed in the second house in Cancer, the equation may become better. The native may possess remarkable singing talent, and he may come across very good amount of success, money, recognition and fame. He may deliver several hit songs, and he may receive many awards. If the finer factors and running times are supportive, he may become one of the most successful singers of his time, and his net worth may be in multimillions.

Taking an example for a female native, suppose benefic combust Moon is placed in the ninth house of a horoscope in Aquarius with Venus, benefic Sun and benefic retrograde Mercury. Benefic Rahu is placed in the first house in Gemini, Ketu is placed in the seventh house in Sagittarius, Mars is placed in the fifth house in Libra, and Saturn is placed in the fourth house in Virgo. Sun and Mercury form Budhaditya Yoga in the ninth house. In this case, the native may become an actor, and she may witness good results.

If benefic retrograde Jupiter is placed in the eleventh house in Aries, the equation may become better. The native may be beautiful, she may possess remarkable acing talent, and she may come across very good amount of success, money, recognition and fame. She may act very well in the genres of romance, drama and comedy. She may deliver several hit movies, and she may receive many awards. If the finer factors and running times are supportive, she may become one of the most successful actors of her time, and her net worth may be in multimillions.

On the other hand, when malefic in nature, combination of Sun and combust Moon in the ninth house of a horoscope in Aquarius can trouble the native with problems related to father, mother, family, wealth, speech, siblings, colleagues, profession, finances, reputation, authority, recognition and several other problems, depending on his/her overall horoscope and running times.

Sun rules the third house, Moon rules the second house, and they are placed in the ninth house. If such combination of Sun and combust Moon is influenced by malefic planets, and/or an overall malefic horoscope, the native may witness various types of problems related to or through his father, mother, family and/or siblings. Considering parents, the native may not have a good equation with his father/mother, his parents may get divorced and he may live with his father/mother, his father/mother may suffer from a long-lasting illness, he/she may be an alcoholic and/or a drug addict, he/she may be a criminal, and/or he/she may die before native's age of 20, depending on native's overall horoscope and running times. Considering siblings, the native may have bad relationships with some of his siblings, and/or he may witness various types of problems through them or due to them. The native may have siblings who may be criminals, and/or drug addicts, and he may face several problems because of them. In an extreme case, the native may lose one or more siblings to death, before his age of 40 or 35.

The native may witness delays, financial losses, setbacks, failures, job loss, bad reputation and several other problems related to or through his profession. Taking an example, suppose combust Moon is placed in the ninth house of a horoscope in Aquarius with Sun, Venus and malefic Rahu. Malefic Ketu is placed in the third house in Leo, malefic Mars is placed in the tenth house in Pisces with debilitated Mercury; retrograde Saturn is placed in the eighth house in Capricorn, and Jupiter is placed in the sixth house in Scorpio. Grahan Yoga is formed in the ninth house.

In this case, native's father may die before native's age of 10 or 5. His mother may get married again, but the native may not have a good equation with his stepfather. The native may not achieve much professional success till his age of 35/40, or throughout his life, though he may earn well at times. He may witness financial losses and bad reputation through profession He may lose one or more siblings to death, before his age of 35 or 30. He may witness 1 or 2 failed marriages.

Combust Moon in Ninth House in Pisces

When Sun and combust Moon are placed in the ninth house of a horoscope in Pisces, Cancer rises in the ascendant. Sun rules the second house, and Moon rules the first house. In general, this combination is benefic here, in most cases. The concept of various planets exhibiting tendencies to be benefic or malefic on the basis of the houses they rule in a horoscope has been explained in the book 'Gemstones: Magic or Science?'.

Combination of Sun and combust Moon in the ninth house of horoscope in Pisces is benefic in most cases, though it may turn malefic in some cases. It may happen when such combination is influenced by one or more malefic planets, and/or an overall malefic horoscope. The concept of a benefic planet turning malefic due to influences of malefic planets has been explained in the book 'Match Making and Manglik Dosh'.

When benefic in nature, combination of Sun and combust Moon in the ninth house of a horoscope in Pisces can bless the native with good results related to father, mother, creativity, spiritual growth, health, lifespan, family, wealth, speech, profession, finances, reputation, authority, recognition, fame and several other good results, depending on his/her overall horoscope and running times.

Such combination of Sun and combust Moon can render various types of benefits to the native, related to or through

his father, mother, family and/or lifespan. Considering parents, native's father/mother may be a rich man/woman, a celebrity, an officer in government or a powerful politician. The native may enjoy many benefits because of his father/mother's money, influence and/or status. He/she may give a big amount of money, and/or wealth to the native, while he/she's alive, and/or through his/her will. Such combination of Sun and combust Moon can render creativity, bravery, courage, leadership abilities and business skills to the native, among other things. Hence, he may achieve success through a wide variety of jobs, and/or businesses. It can also bless the native with good health and a long life, like beyond 70, 80 or 90, depending on his overall horoscope and running times.

Looking at profession, such combust Moon can help the native achieve success as a fire fighter, fitness trainer, body builder, sportsman, athlete, physician, dietician, lawyer, astrologer, tantric, psychic, spiritual guru, healer, religious guru, teacher, preacher, consultant, researcher, analyst, host, artist, poet, chef, interior designer, police officer, army, air force, naval, revenue, administrative, foreign services officer, judge, doctor, scientist, engineer, politician, professional dealing in education industry, coaching, food, health, pharma, medical, nursing, homecare, real estate, agriculture, hospitality, beauty, fashion, finance, television, music, sports, media, book, publishing, fitness, travel, hotel, airline, fishing, shipping, telecom, computer, software, IT, internet industry or some other type of professional, depending on his/her overall horoscope and running times.

Taking an example, suppose benefic combust Moon is placed in the ninth house of a horoscope in Pisces with benefic

Sun and benefic exalted Venus. Benefic exalted Rahu is placed in the eleventh house in Taurus, exalted Ketu is placed in the fifth house in Scorpio, retrograde Mercury is placed in the eighth house in Aquarius, Jupiter is placed in the second house in Leo, and Saturn is placed in the seventh house in Capricorn. In this case, the native may start a company which may deal in packed food products, and he may witness good results.

If benefic debilitated Mars is placed in the first house in Cancer, the equation may become better. In this case, the native may come across very good amount of success, money and recognition through food industry. His business may expand after his age of 35/40, and it may keep growing. If the finer factors and running times are supportive, he may own a business empire worth in billions, by his age of 55/60.

Such combust Moon can help the native achieve success through a creative field as an actor, singer, musician, writer, dancer, sportsman, artist, architect, designer, developer or some other likewise professional. Taking an example, suppose benefic combust Moon is placed in the ninth house of a horoscope in Pisces with benefic Sun and benefic exalted Venus. Retrograde Mercury is placed in the tenth house in Aries, benefic Rahu is placed in the second house in Leo, Ketu is placed in the eighth house in Aquarius, Jupiter is placed in the eleventh house in Taurus, and Saturn is placed in the third house in Virgo. In this case, the native may become a singer, and he may witness good results.

If benefic Mars is placed in the eleventh house in Taurus with Jupiter, the equation may become better. The native may possess remarkable singing talent, and he may come across very good amount of success, money, recognition and fame.

He may deliver several hit songs, and he may receive many awards. He may also write some songs. If the finer factors and running times are supportive, he may become one of the most successful singers of his time, and his net worth may be in multimillions.

On the other hand, when malefic in nature, combination of Sun and combust Moon in the ninth house of a horoscope in Pisces can trouble the native with problems related to father, mother, health, lifespan, family, wealth, speech, profession, finances, reputation, authority, recognition and several other problems, depending on his/her overall horoscope and running times.

Sun rules the second house, Moon rules the first house, and they are placed in the ninth house. If such combination of Sun and combust Moon is influenced by malefic planets, and/or an overall malefic horoscope, the native may witness various types of problems related to or through his father, mother, family and/or lifespan. Considering parents, the native may not have a good equation with his father/mother, his parents may get divorced and he may live with his father/mother, his father/mother may suffer from a long-lasting illness, he/she may be an alcoholic and/or a drug addict, he/she may be a criminal, and/or he/she may die before native's age of 20, depending on native's overall horoscope and running times. Considering lifespan, the native may witness reduction in lifespan due to several reasons. For example, the native may die in an accident, through a natural disaster, due to a fatal disease, due to a fatal viral infection like COVID, due to drug addiction, he may commit suicide, or someone may kill him intentionally or unintentionally. Considering some unintentional incidents, he may get caught in a crossfire between two rival criminal gangs or that between criminals and police, or someone may accidently kill him.

The native may witness delays, financial losses, setbacks, failures, job loss, bad reputation and several other problems related to or through his profession. Taking an example, suppose combust Moon is placed in the ninth house of a horoscope in Pisces with Sun, malefic debilitated Rahu and malefic retrograde Saturn. Malefic debilitated Ketu is placed in the third house in Virgo with retrograde Jupiter; malefic Mercury is placed in the eighth house in Aquarius with Venus; and Mars is placed in the sixth house in Sagittarius. Grahan Yoga is formed in the ninth house whereas Guru Chandal Yoga is formed in the third house.

In this case, native's father as well as mother may die before his age of 10 or 5. He may be adopted by some relatives, or a family through orphanage. He may not achieve much professional success till his age of 35/40, or throughout his life, though he may earn well at times. He may remain jobless for periods of more than 3 months, many times in his life. He may not get married till his age of 35/40, or throughout his life. He may die before his age of 55 or 50, due to some type of cancer, another fatal disease, in an accident, or because of a fatal viral infection like COVID.

Contact Details

Website

www.AstrologerPanditJi.com

Facebook:

https://www.facebook.com/HimanshuShangari

Email IDs:

himanshu1847-himanshushangari@yahoo.com

himanshu1847-astrologerpanditji@yahoo.com

himanshushangari1847@gmail.com

www.ingramcontent.com/pod-product-compliance
Lightning Source LLC
LaVergne TN
LVHW041031150826
845672LV00001B/265